Van Dyck in Check Trousers

1 July to 10 September 1978

held in the

Scottish National Portrait Gallery

Catalogue

1 The Hon Mary Bellenden (d 1736) as *Mary, Queen of Scots*
by Charles Jervas
copy photograph from the original in the collection of the Duke of Argyll

2 Madelina, Baroness Gray (1799–1869) as *Mary, Queen of Scots*
by Sir John Watson Gordon, 1826
oil, 190 × 151 cm
The Hartree Hotel, Biggar

3 Mary Lowther Ferguson (d 1884) as *Mary, Queen of Scots* for Lady Londonderry's ball, 1844
by Julius Jacob, 1844
copy photograph from the original in the collection of John MacLeod of MacLeod

4 Alexandra, Princess of Wales (1844–1925) as *Mary, Queen of Scots* for the Waverley Ball, 1871
by unknown photographer
Scottish National Portrait Gallery

5 Dress worn by Princess Alexandra as *Queen Mary* in 1871, altered later, possibly in 1874 for the Marlborough House Ball
by Elise of Regent Street, London
claret-coloured velvet with sleeves and front of blue-green satin trimmed with gold lace and paste jewels
Museum of London

6 Cartoon on unsuitable figures in fancy dress
by George Du Maurier, 1885
copy photograph from *Punch*

7 Catherine, Duchess of Queensberry (c 1701–1777) as a milkmaid by or after Charles Jervas
oil, 127 × 101 cm
National Portrait Gallery, London

8 Mrs Albinia Hobart (d 1816) as a milkmaid
by James Gillray, 1795
etching, 28·3 × 19·2 cm
British Museum

9 The Abbotsford family as country farmers
by Sir David Wilkie, 1817
oil, 28 × 37·6 cm
Scottish National Portrait Gallery

10 Edward Wortley Montagu (1713–1776) in Eastern dress
by Matthew William Peters
oil, 111·7 × 82·5 cm
National Portrait Gallery, London

11 Edward William (or John) Lane and Mr Lewis in Eastern dress
photograph by David Octavius Hill and Robert Adamson
Scottish National Portrait Gallery

12 Rev John Wilson (1804–1875) in Arab dress
photograph by David Octavius Hill and Robert Adamson
Scottish National Portrait Gallery

13 Sir William Allan (1782–1850) in Circassian dress
by William Nicholson
oil, 91·4 × 71·4 cm
Scottish National Portrait Gallery

14 Miniature Hussar costume used on a lay figure by Arthur Devis
blue satin with pink cuffs and yellow braid trimming
Harris Museum and Art Gallery, Preston

15 Mary Lewis (c 1735–1808) in a seventeenth-century ruff
by William Hogarth, c 1755
oil, 56·8 × 47·5 cm
Aberdeen Art Gallery

16 *A boy in Van Dyck dress*
by Sir Joshua Reynolds
oil, 76·2 × 61 cm
Glasgow Art Gallery

17 Peter, Lord Gwydir (1782–1865) in Vandyckian dress
by Richard Cosway, 1807
pencil and wash, 28 × 21·5 cm
Earl of Ancaster

18 John, Lord Mountstuart (1744–1814) in Vandyckian dress
by Johann Zoffany
oil, 91·5 × 71 cm
Earl of Harrowby

19 Lord Charles Montague as *Charles I*; for the Devonshire House Ball, 1897
copy photograph from *The Devonshire House Fancy Dress Ball*, National Library of Scotland

20 Theodore Napier (b 1845) in 'cavalier highland dress'
by unknown photographer
Scottish National Portrait Gallery

21 Helena (or Suzanne) Fourment
by Sir Peter Paul Rubens
copy photograph from the original in the collection of the Calouste Gulbenkian Foundation, Lisbon

22 Unknown lady with peacock feather
attributed to Allan Ramsay
oil, 123 × 99 cm
Lent anonymously

23 Costume sketch
by Josef Van Haecken
black and white chalk, 39·7 × 35·2 cm
National Gallery of Scotland

24 Costume sketch
by Josef Van Haecken
black and white chalk, 46 × 30·3 cm
National Gallery of Scotland

25 Lady Caroline Ann Macdonald
by Andrew Robertson after John Jackson, 1824
oil miniature, 16·3 cm h
National Museum of Antiquities of Scotland

26 Fashion plate
from *Petit Courrier des Dames*, 1837
Adam Dickson Esq

27 The Hon Mrs Mary Graham (1757–1792)
by Thomas Gainsborough
oil, 237 × 154 cm
National Gallery of Scotland

28 Mary, Duchess of Ancaster (d 1793)
by J McArdell after Thomas Hudson
mezzotint, 50·5 × 35 cm
Scottish National Portrait Gallery

29 Lady Evelyn Ewart as the *Duchess of Ancaster* for the
Devonshire House Ball, 1897
copy photograph from *The Devonshire House Fancy
Dress Ball*, National Library of Scotland

30 *Le Chapeau de Paille*
by Sir Peter Paul Rubens
copy photograph from the original in the National
Gallery, London

31 Sketches from *Le Chapeau de Paille* and for *Summer*
by Andrew Geddes
pastel, 11·8 × 9 and 15·2 × 11·5 cm
National Gallery of Scotland

32 Charlotte Nasmyth (1804–1884) as *Summer*
by Andrew Geddes
oil, 81·3 × 64·2 cm
National Gallery of Scotland

33 Album of sketches for the tableaux held at Hatfield,
1833
by Sir David Wilkie
pen and wash
Marquis of Salisbury

34 Album of costumes for the tableaux held at Hatfield,
1833
attributed to Charlotte, Countess of Verulam
watercolour
Marquis of Salisbury

35 *Mary, Queen of Scots attended by Rizzio*
copy photograph of tableau by Victor Albert Prout,
1863, from an album in the Scottish National
Portrait Gallery

36 *Homage to Queen Victoria*
tableau of the ladies of Queen Victoria's household,
1888
photograph by Byrne and Co
lent by Her Majesty The Queen

37 *Carmen*
tableau with Major Bigge, Prince Henry of Battenberg and Miss Minnie Cochrane, 1888
photograph by Byrne and Co
lent by Her Majesty The Queen

38 *The Casket*
tableau with Princess Alexandra of Edinburgh, Hon
Ethel Cadogan and Hon Harry Legge
by unknown photographer
lent by Her Majesty The Queen

39 *The Three Fishers*
copy photograph of tableau, 1894
from the original photograph in the collection of
Her Majesty The Queen

40 *Harvest*
copy of photograph of tableau by George
Washington Wilson, 1888
from the original photograph in the collection of
Her Majesty The Queen

41 *Malcolm Canmore*
copy of photograph of tableau by George
Washington Wilson, 1888
from the original photograph in the collection of
Her Majesty The Queen

42 *Greek Poetry*
copy of photograph of tableau, 1894
from the original photograph in the collection of
Her Majesty The Queen

43 *An Indian Scene*
copy of photograph of tableau, 1894
from the original photograph in the collection of
Her Majesty The Queen

44 *Charles Edward*
copy of photograph of tableau by George
Washington Wilson, 1888
from the original photograph in the collection of
Her Majesty The Queen

45 *The Sleeping Beauty*
tableau with Princess Alexandra of Edinburgh and
Lord William Cecil, 1890
by unknown photographer
lent by Her Majesty The Queen

46 *A Collection of Engravings from Ancient Vases*
by Johann Wilhelm Tischbein, 1791
Edinburgh University Library

47 *Drawings Faithfully Copied from Nature at Naples*
by Thomas Piroli after Frederick Rehberg
National Library of Scotland

48 Emma, Lady Hamilton (?1761–1815)
by Richard Cosway
pencil and watercolour, 22·3 × 14 cm
National Portrait Gallery, London

49 Lady Hamilton in an attitude
by unknown engraver, 1798
British Museum

50 Unknown historical group
modern print from original negative by David
Octavius Hill and Robert Adamson
Scottish National Portrait Gallery

51 *Edie Ochiltree and Miss Wardour*
with John Henning and Miss Cockburn
photograph by David Octavius Hill and Robert
Adamson
Scottish National Portrait Gallery

52 *The Monks of Kennaquhair*
with William Borthwick Johnstone, William
Leighton Leitch and David Scott
photograph by David Octavius Hill and Robert
Adamson
Scottish National Portrait Gallery

53 *The Monks of Kennaquhair* (2)
with William Borthwick Johnstone and William
Leighton Leitch
photograph by David Octavius Hill and Robert
Adamson
Scottish National Portrait Gallery

54 Unknown man in fancy dress
photograph by David Octavius Hill and Robert
Adamson
Scottish National Portrait Gallery

55 *Don Quixote in his study*
photogravure by William Lake Price
Scottish National Portrait Gallery

56 Thomas Faed (1826–1900)
photograph by David Wilkie Wynfield
National Portrait Gallery, London

57 Sir John Everett Millais (1829–1896) as *Dante*
photograph by David Wilkie Wynfield
National Portrait Gallery, London

58 *Merlin and Vivien*
with Charles Hay Cameron
photograph by Julia Margaret Cameron
National Portrait Gallery, London

59 *Boadicea*
photograph by Julia Margaret Cameron
National Portrait Gallery, London

60 Princess Amelia (1783–1810)
by Peter Edward Stroehling, 1807
oil, 57·1 × 41·6 cm
lent by Her Majesty The Queen

61 Frederica, Countess of Mansfield (1792–1860)
attributed to George Sanders
oil, 75 × 61·5 cm
Earl of Mansfield

62 Lady Charlotte Campbell (1775–1861)
by Johann Wilhelm Tischbein
oil, 197·2 × 134 cm
Scottish National Portrait Gallery

63 William Hamilton of Bangour (1704–1754)
by Gavin Hamilton
oil, 91·5 × 71·1 cm
Scottish National Portrait Gallery

64 Lady Emily Kerr as a *bacchante*
by William Hoare
oil, 177 × 146 cm
Holburne of Menstrie Museum, Bath

65 'Neoclassical' shawl, *c* 1809
muslin with red and beige wool embroidery
Gallery of English Costume, Manchester

66 'Neoclassical' socks, early nineteenth century
buff cotton
Strangers' Hall Museum, Norwich

67 'Neoclassical' fashion plate
from *Costume Parisien*, 1798
Adam Dickson Esq

68 'Neoclassical' fashion plate
from *Costume Parisien*, 1803
Adam Dickson Esq

69 Unknown lady as a sorceress
by Richard Cosway, 1805
pencil and wash, 36·8 × 28·9 cm
Duke of Hamilton

70 The Hon Mrs Thomas Hope in a 'Grecian' dress
after George Dawe
mezzotint, 59·7 × 38·1 cm
Scottish National Portrait Gallery

71 *Costume of the Ancients*
by Thomas Hope, 1809
Edinburgh University Library

72 Alderman John Sawbridge (?1732–1795)
by Thomas Watson after Benjamin West
mezzotint, 51·3 × 37 cm
Scottish National Portrait Gallery

73 *Form versus Fashion*
satire by Gourlay Steell junior, 1885
watercolour and pencil, 35·2 × 25·4 cm
Scottish National Portrait Gallery

74 Advertisement for Liberty and Co
Savoy theatre programme, 6 July 1889
Theatre Museum, Victoria and Albert Museum

75 Satire on neoclassical attitudes
by George Du Maurier
copy photograph from *Punch*, 1878

76 Advertisements for Sanatogen
from *Illustrated London News*, 1930s

77 Advertisement for Cramp's patent stocking
suspenders
copy photograph from Marie Schild, *Album of Fancy
Costumes*

78 'Neoclassical' dress, *c* 1809
white muslin embroidered with sequins, silver thread
and white silk
Victoria and Albert Museum

79 Dress by Liberty Costumes, *c* 1890
white silk
Birmingham City Museum

80 Dress by Marius Fortuny, early twentieth century
pale olive-green, mushroom-pleated silk
Royal Scottish Museum

81 Costume worn by Thomas, Lord Binning, as a Privy
Councillor at the coronation of George IV, 1821
blue silk trimmed with gold braid and sequins
National Museum of Antiquities of Scotland

82 Queen Charlotte with her sons, George, Prince of
Wales and Frederick, Duke of York
by Johann Zoffany
copy photograph from the original in the collection
of Her Majesty The Queen

83 Danish fancy dress worn at the Prince Regent's fête
plate from *La Belle Assemblée*, August 1819
Adam Dickson Esq

84 *The Challenge* at the coronation of George IV
coloured lithograph by unknown artist
British Museum

85 Restoration-style dress worn by Queen Victoria in
1851
grey watered silk trimmed with gold and silver,
underskirt of cloth of gold
Museum of London

86 Queen Victoria and Prince Albert in Restoration
dress, 1851
by Franz Xavier Winterhalter
watercolour, 55·9 × 44·4 cm
lent by Her Majesty The Queen

87 Prince Albert (1819–1861) in eighteenth-century
dress, 1845
by J Brandard
lithograph, 30 × 20·9 cm
Adam Dickson Esq

88 Queen Victoria and Prince Albert as Queen Philippa
and Edward III, 1842
by Sir Edwin Landseer
oil, 131 × 111 cm
lent by Her Majesty The Queen

89 The Hon Hugh Cholmondeley as *Sir Damian De Lacy*
for the Waverley Quadrille at the 1842 royal ball
probably by Frederick Coke Smyth
watercolour, 43·2 × 33 cm
Michael Clayton Esq

90 Arthur, Duke of Connaught (1850–1942) as *The
Beast* for the Fairy Tale Quadrille at the Marlborough House Ball, 1874
copy photograph from the original in the collection
of Her Majesty The Queen

91 Edward, Prince of Wales (1841–1910) as the *Lord of
the Isles* for the Waverley Ball, 1871
by unknown photographer
Scottish National Portrait Gallery

92 Alexandra, Princess of Wales (1844–1925) as
Marguerite de Valois for the Devonshire House Ball
photograph by Lafayette
lent by Her Majesty The Queen

93 The Duke and Duchess of York at the Devonshire
House Ball
photograph by Lafayette
lent by Her Majesty The Queen

94 E A Walton and Helen Law as *Hokusai and Whistler's
Butterfly*, 1889
by Sir John Lavery
oil, 60 × 45·5 cm
Mrs Dorothy Walton

95 *Costumes d'Ivanhoe*, 1823
lithographs by Jobard after Felicité Lagarenne
National Library of Scotland

96 *Soldat aux Gardes*
by de Frey after Paul Gavarni
lithograph, 32·5 × 23·4 cm
Adam Dickson Esq

97 Fashion plate from *Le Moniteur de la Mode*
by Jules David
hand tinted engraving, 26·2 × 18·1 cm
Adam Dickson Esq

98 Fashion plate from *La Mode Illustrée*, 1872
by Avais Coudouse after Huard
hand tinted engraving, 36·1 × 26·7 cm
Adam Dickson Esq

99 The Master of Herries dressed for the Waverley Ball,
1871
by unknown photographer
lent by Her Majesty The Queen

100 Lady Archibald Campbell as *Jeanie Deans* for the
Waverley Ball
by unknown photographer
lent by Her Majesty The Queen

101 The Hon Oliver Montagu as *Richard Coeur de Lion*(?)
for the Waverley Ball
by unknown photographer
lent by Her Majesty The Queen

102 Count Maffei dressed for the Waverley Ball
by unknown photographer
lent by Her Majesty The Queen

103 Fashion plate from *Petit Courrier des Dames*, 1836
by unknown engraver
hand tinted engraving, 22·7 × 14·2 cm
Adam Dickson Esq

104 Fashion plate from *L'Iris*, 1857
by Louis Berli after Heloise Leloir
hand tinted engraving, 27·9 × 19·6 cm
Adam Dickson Esq

105 Clementina Stirling Graham (1782–1877) as an old
lady
by unknown artist
watercolour, 21·3 × 16·2 cm
Scottish National Portrait Gallery

106 Fashion plate from *Der Bazar*, 1895
by H B G
hand tinted engraving, 38·6 × 29 cm
Adam Dickson Esq

107 Fashion plate from *Societé Generale des Journaux de
Modes Professionels*, 1904
by 'Cleo'
lithograph, 38 × 26 cm
Adam Dickson Esq

108 Fashion plate from *Courrier de la Mode*
by unknown engraver
hand tinted engraving, 27·3 × 39 cm
Adam Dickson Esq

109 *Fancy Dresses Described*, 1882
by Ardern Holt
Adam Dickson Esq

110 *Gentleman's Fancy Dress*, 1882
by Ardern Holt
Adam Dickson Esq

111 The Glasgow Arts Club Ball, 1889
photograph by J Craig Annan
John Craig Annan (negative)

112 *Les Travestis dans le Parc*
by Pierre Brissaud
from *Gazette du Bon Ton*, September 1913
Adam Dickson Esq

113 William, 3rd Viscount Courtenay (1768–1835)
by Richard Cosway, 1791
oil, 230 × 172 cm
Earl of Devon

114 Mid eighteenth-century dress worn by Isabella
Mowbray Cadell at the St Andrew Boat Club Ball,
c 1897
white ribbed and figured silk brocaded with poly-
chrome silks, nineteenth-century black silk mittens
and underskirt
Mrs Anne Nimmo

115 Guests at the St Andrew Boat Club Ball, *c* 1897
photograph by J Horsburgh
Mrs Anne Nimmo

116 *Portrait of a boy in red*
by unknown Italian artist
copy photograph from the original in the National
Gallery, London

117 Sixteenth-century style costume based on no 116
red silk and dark blue velvet trimmed with gold braid
*Earl of Crawford and Balcarres, on loan to Glasgow
Museum*

118 Fancy dress worn by David, Master of Lindsay and
probably by the Hon James Lindsay
red silk trimmed with gold braid, with silk brocade
tabard
*Earl of Crawford and Balcarres, on loan to Glasgow
Museum*

119 David, Master of Lindsay (1871–1940)
miniature by Reginald Easton, 1876
copy photograph from the original in the collection
of the Earl of Crawford and Balcarres

120 Seventeenth-century style costume worn by the Earl of Gifford, c 1900
by L and H Nathan
cream silk trimmed with gold braid
National Museum of Antiquities of Scotland

121 Dress worn by the Duchess of Portland as the *Duchess of Savoy* at the Devonshire House Ball, 1897
silver satin, the pattern outlined in pearls, brilliants and silver strips, lace ruff; the train and embroidered sleeves are now missing
Victoria and Albert Museum

122 Winifred, Duchess of Portland as the *Duchess of Savoy*
copy photograph from *The Devonshire House Fancy Dress Ball*, National Library of Scotland

123 Costumes worn at the Devonshire House Ball, 1897
copy photographs from *The Devonshire House Fancy Dress Ball*, National Library of Scotland

124 Costume worn by Edward, Prince of Wales as *Grand Prior of the Order of St John of Jerusalem* at the Devonshire House Ball, 1897
by Alias, 36 Soho Square, London
doublet and trunk hose of black velvet with bead embroidery, black velvet cloak, silk hat, boots, sword belt and sword
Bermans and Nathans Ltd

125 Edward, Prince of Wales (1841–1910) as *Grand Prior*
copy photograph from *The Devonshire House Fancy Dress Ball*, National Library of Scotland

126–9 *General View of the Lists, The Joust, The Mêlée* and *The Presentation of the Knight*
lithographs by K Loeillot after James Henry Nixon from John Richardson, *The Eglinton Tournament*, 1843
Scottish National Portrait Gallery

130 *The Tournament at Eglinton Castle*, 1840
lithographs by Edward Corbould
National Library of Scotland

131 *An Account of the Tournament at Eglinton. . .*
by James Aikman, illustrated by W Gordon, 1839
Adam Dickson Esq

132 Armour, horse trappings and lance used by George, Lord Glenlyon (later 6th Duke of Atholl) as *Knight of the Gael* at the Eglinton Tournament
supplied by Samuel Pratt
Duke of Atholl

133 George, 6th Duke of Atholl (1814–1864), wearing his tournament armour
by Stewart Watson, 1846
oil, c 120 × 90 cm
Duke of Atholl

134 Armour worn by Captain J O Fairlie as the *Knight of the Golden Lion* at the Eglinton Tournament
composite suit of French and German armour made by Samuel Pratt (the nineteenth-century paint has recently been cleaned off)
Captain D O Fairlie

135 Captain J O Fairlie of Coodham in his tournament armour
by unknown photographer, c 1850
Captain D O Fairlie

136 J O R Fairlie of Myres in the evening dress worn by his father at the Eglinton Tournament
by F Guidi, Rome, 1870
oil, c 100 × 60 cm
Captain D O Fairlie

137 Charles Kinnaird Sheridan (d 1847) in the armour he wore as a spectator at the Eglinton Tournament
by unknown artist
oil, 45·5 × 35 cm
Tower Armouries

138 Lady Elizabeth Seymour as the *Queen of Beauty*
by J Bouvier
lithograph, 40·7 × 24·8 cm
National Portrait Gallery, London

139 Costume worn by John Balfour of Balbirnie (1811–1895) as esquire to Viscount Glenlyon at the Eglinton Tournament
silk tartan tunic and bonnet
Mr J C and Dr Jean Balfour of Balbirnie

140 Costume worn by John Balfour of Balbirnie for the ball held during the Eglinton Tournament
tunic of green plush trimmed with silk and metal braid, undertunic of crimson damask woven with metal threads, cream cotton shirt, buff boots
Mr J C and Dr Jean Balfour of Balbirnie

141 The Eglinton Tournament trophy presented to the Earl to commemorate the event
designed by Edmund Cotterill and made by Garrard, London
silver, c 1 metre high
Earl of Eglinton

142 Sir Francis Sykes and family
by Daniel Maclise, c 1837
watercolour, 113 × 64·8 cm
F J B Sykes Esq

143 William Black (1841–1898)
by John Pettie, 1877
oil, 128·3 × 80 cm
Glasgow Art Gallery

Van Dyck in Check Trousers

Artists have to wrestle today with the horrible antagonism of modern dress; no wonder, therefore, that few recent portraits look really dignified. Just imagine Vandyck's 'Charles I' in a pair of check trousers!

J E Millais

Arthur, Duke of Connaught (1850–1942) as the *Beast* for the Fairy Tale Quadrille at the Marlborough House Ball, 1874, by unknown photographer
reproduced by gracious permission of Her Majesty The Queen

Van Dyck in Check Trousers

Fancy Dress in Art and Life
1700–1900

Sara Stevenson
of the Scottish National
Portrait Gallery

Helen Bennett
of the National Museum of
Antiquities of Scotland

Scottish National Portrait Gallery
The Trustees of the National Galleries of Scotland
1978

ISBN 0 903148 16 1

Contents

*Sara Stevenson
†Helen Bennett

Acknowledgements

We are grateful to all those who have kindly permitted us to reproduce their pictures and costumes and to the following who have supplied us with help and information: Mr Ian Anstruther; Miss Janet Arnold; Mr Michael Clayton; Mr John Gudenian of Bermans and Nathans Ltd; Miss Elspeth Evans, Mr Colin Ford, Mr John Kerslake and Miss K R Poole of the National Portrait Gallery, London; Miss Kay Staniland and Mrs Valerie Cumming of the Museum of London; Mrs M B Ginsberg of the Victoria and Albert Museum, London; Miss Sarah Barter Bailey of the Tower Armouries; Miss Frances Dimond of the Royal Archives; Mr Oliver Fairclough of the City of Birmingham Museums; Mrs Vanda Foster of the Gallery of English Costumes, Manchester; Miss Fiona Strodder of the Norwich County Museum Service; Mr Roger Billcliffe, Mr Brian Blench and Miss Jane Tozer of the Glasgow Museums and Art Gallery; Miss Naomi Tarrant of the Royal Scottish Museum, Edinburgh.

Our particular thanks are due to Mr Adam Dickson, Chairman of the Costume Society, for constant help and advice.

We are also indebted to our colleagues for their assistance, especially Miss Christine Haddow.

Modern Dress & Fancy Portraits

For the whole of the eighteenth century and up until about 1830, British painting was almost entirely monopolised by the production of portraits and patronage for any other kind of painting was rare. The whole period echoes with cries of frustration: 'This cursed portrait painting! How am I shackled with it!'[1] Many of the artists engaged in portrait painting, even the most successful, felt themselves tied to a lower art form when they would have preferred to paint historical or literary scenes or landscapes and to choose their own subjects, arrange them to their own taste, and paint their own imagined ideal rather than the often intractable truth. This, not unnaturally, resulted in the attempt to bend portraiture towards the ideal and the historical and away from the strictly limiting truth.

One of the biggest objections to the practice of portraiture was contemporary dress. However glamorous the costume of the eighteenth and nineteenth centuries looks to us now, at the time it was commonplace. If the artist worked on it in detail, all his hard work went into producing something ordinary and after a short space of time it would look old-fashioned and make the painting and the sitter ridiculous. Even the paintings of Sir Joshua Reynolds, who went to considerable trouble to try to achieve a compromise 'timeless' form of dress, were criticised in the 1820s for this same lapse into unfashionability. 'Nevertheless, Sir Joshua's pictures, seen among standard works, have (to speak it plainly) something old-womanish about them. By their obsolete and affected air they remind one of antiquated ladies of quality, and are a kind of Duchess-Dowagers in the art— somewhere between the living and the dead.'[2] The desire to achieve timelessness in portraiture was continued throughout the two hundred years from 1700 to 1900. In the *Spectator* of 1711, the same hope is expressed: 'Great Masters in Painting never care for drawing People in the Fashion, as very well knowing that the Head-dress, or Periwig, that now prevails, and gives a Grace to their Portraitures at present, will make a very odd Figure, and perhaps look monstrous in the Eyes of Posterity. For this reason they often represent an illustrious Person in a *Roman* habit or some other dress that never varies.'[3]

The author of this piece in the *Spectator* was plainly not hostile to modern dress but the dislike of contemporary clothing and fashions was a perpetual complaint in the mouths of artists who generally agreed with Millais that the artists of the past, like Van Dyck, had the great advantage of more picturesque costume to paint. Allan Cunningham attacked the dress of the early nineteenth century when talking about the difficulties experienced by Thomas Lawrence at the beginning of his career: 'He had not then learned the art in which he afterwards became a master, of softening down the geometrical lines and manifold points of modern dress into something like elegance; the broad and innumerable buttons; the close-fitted capes; the peaked lapels, and hanging cuffs, and pointed skirts of these our latter days are sorely in the way of a young artist who thinks of Michael Angelo and the antique, and dreams of his profession like a poet. Nor were the dresses of the women less extravagant than those of the men; their hair frizzed, and filled with pomatum and powder; a wide hat, and enormous feather stuck on top of the head; a close cut riding jacket, wide at the shoulders, and pinched at the waist so tightly, that, with the expanding petticoat and spreading hat, they looked like sand-glasses, and were, assuredly, sad frights, either in life or painting.'[4] Later in the century George Frederic Watts was of the opinion that Victorian dress, especially for men, was so appalling that portrait painting could no longer be high art: 'Portraiture...is deprived (speaking of masculine portraits) of nearly all that from an artistic point of view can render it valuable to posterity... The ugliness of most things connected with our ordinary habits is most remarkable. A well-dressed gentleman ready for dinner or attired for any ceremony is a pitiable example—his vesture nearly formless and quite foldless if he can have his will. His legs, unshapen props—his shirt front, a void—his dress coat, an unspeakable piece of ignobleness.'[5] Lady Elizabeth Eastlake, who approved of the women's dress of 1850, agreed with Watts' opinion of male dress, 'the male

costume being reduced to a mysterious combination of the inconvenient and the unpicturesque, which, except in the light of a retribution, it is puzzling to account for.'[6]

A reasonably large body of public opinion was in agreement with the artists, both in the concern that the portrait should not become unfashionable and in the belief that contemporary dress was dull, although many who had never thought about the question may have been persuaded into that view by the artists. The result was the 'fancy' portrait. The fancy portrait dressed the sitter in foreign, classical, historical, or rustic dress to give a properly timeless quality to the painting and the artist was thus enabled to indulge in flowing draperies, exotic colours, and eccentric attitudes and movements not permissible in everyday dress. There is no doubt that the pleasure of the artist in the unusual freedom of this kind of portraiture means that the fancy dress portraits of the eighteenth and nineteenth centuries include a high proportion of the most splendid and appealing portraits of the time.

The fancy portrait did, unfortunately, present more problems in achieving a likeness, which remained of considerable interest to the sitter. In a case where the sitter, Lady Dartmouth, had expressed a preference for a fancy portrait and then rejected the result as unlike, Thomas Gainsborough attempted to throw all the blame on the costume: 'I only for the present beg your Lordship will give me leave to try an Experiment upon that Picture to prove the amazing Effect of dress—I mean to treat it as a cast off Picture and dress it (contrary I know to Lady Dartmouth's taste) in the modern way; the worst consequence that can attend it will be Her Ladyship's being angry with me for a time—I am vastly out in my notion of the thing if the face does not immediately look like... My Lord I am very well aware of the Objection to modern dresses in Pictures, that they are soon out of fashion & look awkward; but as that misfortune cannot be helped we must set it against the unluckiness of fancied dresses taking away Likenesses, the principal beauty and intention of a Portrait... Had a picture voice, action, etc to make itself known, as Actors have upon the Stage, no disguise would be sufficient to conceal a person; but only a face, confined to one View, and not a muscle to move to say, "Here I am", falls very hard upon the poor Painter who perhaps is not within a mile of the truth in painting the Face only...'[7] In fact, Gainsborough was in this instance making excuses for a bad painting, and several of his most popular portraits like *The Blue Boy* and the *Hon Mrs Graham* (*ill 24*) are fancy portraits derived from just such a 'fictitious bundle of trumpery'.

The dramatic and distinguished effects achieved in fancy portraiture set fashions in portraiture and in the wearing of fancy dress at balls. In turn, many of the fancy portraits show the sitter in actual fancy dress worn for a party. The influence of dress on art and art on dress was a continuous process and it is not always possible to tell whether a dress was real or an artist's invention. This was further complicated between 1770 and 1830 by the tendency of ordinary dress to adopt features of fancy dress. Costumes frequently turn up at second or third hand. For example, Millais' *Cherry Ripe*, the immensely popular sentimental picture of a winsome little girl in a mob cap, shows her in a costume which she wore to a fancy dress ball copied from Joshua Reynolds' painting of Penelope Boothby. Lady Evelyn Ewart went to the Devonshire House Ball in 1897 dressed as Thomas Hudson's painting of the Duchess of Ancaster (*ill 26*), whose costume ultimately derives from Rubens' painting of Helena Fourment.

The 1897 ball, where most of the costumes were based on paintings, was a tribute to the influence of art over fancy dress. But fancy dress could be an art form, albeit often a misguided one, in its own right. The detailed fancy dress books of the 1880s contained such fantasies as:
'EXPRESS. Trained skirt of steel-coloured satin, edged and bound with black velvet, showing a series of rails in steel braid; skirt stiff at back, the hem edged with a row of movable wheels, which must turn at every move of the wearer. The front of the skirt is of black velvet, striped downwards; steel-coloured cuirass; miniature steam engine in hair, with grey feathers issuing from the funnel; flowing

hair and wheeled skates for shoes.'[8] This idea may have had a theatrical origin and is certainly the forerunner of the more lavish Hollywood spectacles. More closely allied to surrealist art is the following suggestion:
'HALL. The figure made to represent a hat-stand with pegs, candlesticks, etc. Skirt of black and white checks to resemble oilcloth; a lamp in the hand. One of the realistic characters so much in favour of late.'[9]

Many artists were interested in masquerades, set up tableaux, and appeared at balls with almost as much enthusiasm as they painted, and some like Sir William Allan brought back exotic costumes from abroad which they wore for portraits, for parties, and lent to others for the same purposes. Others like Richard Cosway took a naturally vain interest in clothes which led, among other eccentricities, to him appearing at sale-rooms in 'a mulberry silk coat profusely embroidered with gold lace and strawberries'.[10] The connection of artists with fancy dress was by no means an academic one. As a result, certain trends and fashions stand out in fancy dress and there is a considerable coincidence between the costume in fancy portraits and that worn at fancy parties.

2
Alexandra, Princess of Wales
(1844–1925) as *Mary,*
Queen of Scots
for the Waverley Ball, 1871
by unknown photographer
Scottish National Portrait Gallery

4

The wish to be a king or a queen is a desire which a surprising number of people carry over from the dim fantasies of childhood into adult life. Fancy portraits, as well as fancy dress parties, showed a large number of people indulging themselves in being royal and all-powerful as such prominent monarchs as Henry VIII, Cleopatra or Mary, Queen of Scots among many others. One of the great charms of fancy dress was that it permitted the indulgence of vanity to an inordinate extent.

Mary, Queen of Scots was the most popular queen in fancy dress terms for the eighteenth and nineteenth centuries. The earliest fashion for imitating her came in the time of Queen Anne. When the 'Orkney' portrait miniature which had triggered off this fashion was sold in 1745, George Vertue recorded: 'this is the original limning which the Duke of Hamilton had recovered and valued most extremely—showd it at Court and everywhere for the genuine picture of the Queen everywhere from thence it was coppyd in water colours enamel many and many times for all persons pining after it thousands of ill immitated coppyes—spread everywhere—this the picture itself—tho amended by or repaired by L Crosse who was ordered to make it as beautifull as he coud—by the Duke.'[11] At that time, and for some years later, many ladies had themselves painted in imitation of the 'Orkney' miniature, and Bernard Lens is said to have made a considerable trade of painting these portraits. The portrait of Mary Bellenden by Charles Jervas is the most dramatic and blatant of these imitations, a full-length portrait, invented from the chest downwards and completely dwarfing the original. The dress was also common at masquerades. Horace Walpole reported a ball in 1742 where the popularity of Mary as a subject for masquerade dress was demonstrated by 'dozens of ugly Queens of Scots'.[12]

The nineteenth century seized on Mary with even more enthusiasm. In 1826 Madelina, Baroness Gray had herself painted as a romantic Mary, Queen of Scots by John Watson Gordon in a dress that she had probably worn at a ball (*ill 1*). In 1828 the Duchesse de Berri, who was a considerable

1 Madelina, Baroness Gray (1799–1869) as *Mary, Queen of Scots*
by Sir John Watson Gordon, 1826
oil, 190 × 151 cm
The Hartree Hotel, Biggar

"WHO'D HAVE THOUGHT IT?"

1885.

"I'M MARY, QUEEN OF SCOTS, AS YOU *SEE*, DR. SQUILLS! AND WHO ARE YOU?" "I'M HORACE WALPOLE!"

3 Satire on the enthusiasm for dressing up as *Mary, Queen of Scots*
by George Du Maurier
from *Punch*, 1885

leader of fashion in France, gave a magnificent fancy dress ball in the Tuileries, based on the Valois court during the time of Mary's presence as the Dauphin's bride.[13] The Duchesse, who particularly admired Mary, took her part at the ball. Alexandra, Princess of Wales attended the Waverley Ball of 1871 as Mary (*ill 2*). By the 1880s the overabundance of women following this fashionable example was beginning to attract mild satire, although Ardern Holt's book *Fancy Dresses Described* had an account of no less than four possible costumes for Mary, Queen of Scots. A fictional account of a fancy ball published in 1888, where the heroines of the day came as Cleopatra and Titania, describes the general scene: 'cavaliers were far too prevalent, Scottish queens were a drug, and monks and Chinamen numerous enough to suggest a run on cheap attire'.[14] It is undoubtedly significant that George Du Maurier's cartoon of an elderly and unappealing couple dressed in inappropriate clothes should show the lady dressed as Mary (*ill 3*).

The reasons for this continuing interest are, firstly, that Mary was kept in the public eye throughout most of the two hundred years by historians arguing whether she was right and virtuous or wrong and wicked, and her adherence to the Roman Catholic faith made the argument considerably more intense. Secondly, Mary, Queen of Scots had the reputation during her lifetime and after of being both beautiful and passionate. Her popularity during the nineteenth century probably rests more on the second than on the first point. The publication of Schiller's *Maria Stuart* in 1800 and Walter Scott's *The Abbot* in 1820 saw the Queen presented more as a

fallible woman with considerable charms than as an absolute black or white historical argument. Where there were many women who would have happily sailed into a ballroom as a desirable and beautiful queen, I very much doubt whether even a few would have expressly wished to appear as a Roman Catholic martyr. Walter Scott refused to write a historical biography of Mary because he said he could not persuade his heart to listen to his head on the subject, and his account of her in *The Abbot* certainly emphasised the beauty and desirability: 'Who is there, that at the very mention of Mary Stewart's name, has not her countenance before him, familiar as that of the mistress of his youth, or the favourite daughter of his advanced age? Even those who feel themselves compelled to believe all, or much, of what her enemies laid to her charge, cannot think without a sigh upon a countenance expressive of anything rather than the foul crimes with which she was charged when living, and which still continue to shade, if not to blacken, her memory. That brow, so truly open and regal—those eyebrows, so regularly graceful, which yet were saved from the charge of regular insipidity by the beautiful effect of the hazel eyes which they over-arched, and which seemed to utter a thousand histories—the nose, with all its Grecian precision of outline—the mouth, so well proportioned, so sweetly formed, as if designed to speak nothing but what was delightful to hear—the dimpled chin—the stately swan-like neck, form a countenance, the like of which we know not to have existed in any other character moving in that high class of life, where the actresses as well as the actors command general and undivided attention.'[15]

In fact, the portraits of Mary are largely disappointing and most of the nineteenth-century imitators copied the spurious or historical pictures rather than the authentic portraits. Scott's opinion alone, however, made the subject worth copying in the hope of borrowing a little second-hand lustre for an evening at a ball or several lifetimes on canvas. It is notable that in several of the major balls, Mary, Queen of Scots turns up as a character out of Scott's novel rather than a historical individual: in the Waverley Quadrille at the Marchioness of Londonderry's ball of 1844 (*ill 4*) and at the Waverley Ball of 1871, for example.

4 Mary Lowther Ferguson (d 1884) as *Mary, Queen of Scots* for Lady Londonderry's ball, 1844
by Julius Jacob, 1844
watercolour, 55.9 × 40.5 cm
John MacLeod of MacLeod

Pastoral Dress

6 Catherine, Duchess of Queensberry (*c* 1701–1777)
as a milkmaid by or after Charles Jervas
oil, 127 × 101 cm
National Portrait Gallery, London

While commoners and aristocrats enjoyed playing at being kings and queens, in the eighteenth century the French Queen was playing at being a milkmaid. The taste for a dream idyllic pastoral life was equally strong in eighteenth-century Britain. Shepherds and shepherdesses were a common feature of masquerades and equally common in portraits. Horace Walpole, who is a useful guide to the social behaviour of the second half of the century, has frequent accounts of Arcadian entertainments, which remained popular despite the climate. He described the failure of several of these parties, one at Stowe in June 1770: 'With a little exaggeration I could make you believe that nothing ever was so delightful. The idea was really pretty; but as my feelings have lost something of their romantic sensibility, I did not quite enjoy such an entertainment *al fresco* so much as I should have done twenty years ago. The evening was more than cool, and the destined spot anything but dry. There were not half lamps enough, and no music but an ancient militia-man, who played cruelly on a squeaking tabor and pipe. As our procession descended the vast flight of steps into the garden, in which was assembled a crowd of people from Buckingham and the neighbouring villages to see the Princess and the show, the moon shining very bright, I could not help laughing as I surveyed our troop, which instead of tripping lightly to such an Arcadian entertainment, were hobbling down by the balustrades, wrapped up in cloaks and great-coats, for fear of catching cold. The Earl, you know, is bent double, the Countess very lame; I am a miserable walker, and the Princess, though as strong as a Brunswick lion, makes no figure in going down fifty stone stairs. Except Lady Anne [Howard], and by courtesy Lady Mary [Coke], we were none of us young enough for a pastoral. We supped in the grotto, which is as proper to this climate as a sea-coal fire would be in the dog-days at Tivoli.'[16]

The same period saw a passion for amateur hay-making. In June 1764, Walpole reported another disastrous occasion: 'The haymaking at Wandsworth-hill did not succeed, from the excessive cold of the night; I proposed to

bring one of the cocks into the great room, and make a bonfire. All the beauties were disappointed, and all the Macaronies afraid of getting the toothache.'[17] Hay was undoubtedly thought to be picturesque. Walpole reports on another occasion leaving the hay out for a few extra days so that his guests could enjoy looking at it. Inevitably, it was rained on. Unfortunately, we have no record of the farmers' opinions on this incompetent and fun-loving way of ruining the harvest.

The portrait of Catherine, Duchess of Queensberry by Charles Jervas, probably of about 1730, shows her as a milkmaid (*ill 6*). The Duchess was not, however, merely dressed up for a masquerade. She was a strong-minded woman, sometimes offensively so, with decided views on dress. She habitually wore a simple country dress with an apron and annoyed the court by turning up at the grand Drawing Rooms dressed in this manner. When an edict was issued, directed at her, forbidding the wearing of aprons at court, she tore off the apron and stamped on in, still in the basic country dress. She did not, of course, habitually carry around a milk pail, nor did she wish to be taken for a simple country maiden. On one occasion, when her husband was attending a military review, she turned up in her usual dress and tried to reach him through the crowd but one of the soldiers, who did not recognise her, pushed her back. The Duchess was so angry that she was only satisfied when the Duke promised to flog the guard in revenge for the insult. The Duchess of Queensberry was able to take this aggresive attitude to dress because she was a very handsome woman. Her approach to dress was not just a desire for simplicity so much as a

wish to please herself. Mrs Delany recorded another occasion when she went to the opposite extreme and dressed herself as a complete rural landscape in a costume of 'white satin embroidered, the bottom of the petticoat *brown hills* covered with all sorts of weeds and *every breadth* had *an old stump of a tree* that ran up almost to the top of the petticoat,... round which twined nasturtersians, ivy, honeysuckles, periwinkles, convolvuluses and all sorts of twining flowers which spread and covered the petticoat, vines with the leaves variegated as you have seen them by the sun...'[18]

Mrs Albinia Hobart, who gave rustic fêtes on Ham Common in the 1790s, was not in the same class of beauty as the Duchess of Queensberry. Her rotund form was an open invitation to Gillray, who satirised her several times, but she was, despite her shape, a good dancer and a good actress. Gillray's caricature illustrated here (*ill 7*) shows her taking part in a rustic play but it is reminiscent of a party she organised in 1791, described again by Horace Walpole: 'It froze hard last night. I went out for a moment to look at my hay-makers, and was starved. The contents of an English June are, hay and ice, orange-flowers and rheumatisms! I am now cowering over the fire. Mrs Hobart had announced a rural breakfast at Sans-Souci last Saturday; nothing being so pastoral as a fat grandmother in a row of houses on Ham Common. It rained early in the morning: she despatched post-boys, for want of Cupids and zephyrs, to stop her nymphs and shepherds who tend their flocks in Pall Mall and St James's-street; but half of them missed the couriers and arrived...'[19] Mrs Hobart introduced this

Enter COWSLIP, with a bowl of Cream... Vide Brandenburg Theatricals.

'As a Cedar tall & slender; — 'Is her nom'tive case.
'Sweet Cowslips Grace — 'And she's of the feminine gender'

7 Mrs Albinia Hobart (d 1816) as a milkmaid
by James Gillray, 1795
etching, 28.3 × 19.2 cm
British Museum

disastrous party, with the rain falling into the cream, into a short play she later wrote called *Le Poulet*, which was acted at Brandenburgh House.

In 1817, David Wilkie painted the group portrait of Sir Walter Scott and his relatives as a Lowland farmer and his family (*ill 8*). This picture had nothing to do with a secret desire by Scott to be a simple farmer; he expressed his views on this very clearly: 'Farming I hate; what have I to do with fattening and killing beasts, or raising corn only to cut it down, and to wrangle with farmers about prices, and to be constantly at the mercy of the seasons?'[20] Wilkie was, of course, famous for his genre paintings and Sir Walter was also famous for his vivid descriptions of common life in Scotland. Wilkie, writing a letter from Carlsbad in 1826, refers to the local reaction to Scott's works: 'The Waverley Novels, as familiar to them as to us, have made our native country, in their eyes, the Arcadia of Europe...'[21] It is probable from this that, at least in part, David Wilkie intended to present Sir Walter and his family as a group that might have stepped out of one of his books. Scott's ideals may be read into the picture, not in any desire for the farming life, but in his passionate interest in the family and the clan as a social unit. According to his son-in-law, 'Fancy rebuilt and most prodigally embellished the whole system of the social existence of the middle ages, in which the clansman (wherever there were clans) ac-knowledged practically no sovereign but his chief. The author of "the Lay" would rather have seen his heir carry the Banner of Bellenden gallantly at a foot-ball match on Carterhaugh, than he would have heard that

the boy had attained the highest honours of the first university in Europe. His original pride was to be an acknowledged member of one of the 'honourable families' whose progenitors had been celebrated by Satchels for following this banner in blind obedience to the patriarchal leader; his first and last worldly ambition was to be himself the founder of a distinct branch; he desired to plant a lasting root, and dreamt not of personal fame, but of

8 The Abbotsford family as country farmers
by Sir David Wilkie, 1817
oil, 28 × 37.6 cm
Scottish National Portrait Gallery

long distant generations rejoicing in the name of "Scott of Abbotsford".[22] The tight knit family group, Scott's eminently patriarchal pose, and the emphasis on the Lowland landscape the figures occupy, all contain visual elements of these attitudes.

10 Edward Wortley Montagu (1713–1776) in Eastern
dress
by Matthew William Peters
oil, 111.7 × 82.5 cm
National Portrait Gallery, London

To the British, true romance and glamour has always come from abroad. Foreign costume has always excited interest for its strangeness and sometimes its beauty. The immense popularity of Hussar dress in the eighteenth century, which led eventually to its adoption by the army and the formation of Hussar regiments, stemmed originally from the fame of the Hungarian soldiers at the battle of Dettingen in 1743. Hussar dress became one of the most common masquerade dresses from this time and doubtless the flamboyance of the costume, with its elaborate gold braiding, helped to maintain its popularity. Both men and boys appear in paintings in the uniform and Arthur Devis had made two small Hussar outfits (*ill 9*) to use on lay figures when painting portraits.[23]

The eighteenth- and nineteenth-century interest in rich colours and flowing lines found most satisfaction in Eastern dress. Visitors to the East found it hard to resist the exotic costumes and often brought them back home. The portrait of Edward Wortley Montagu by Matthew William Peters shows how much the painting benefitted in terms of colour and shape from his dress (*ill 10*). Montagu, whose own mother described him as 'an excellent linguist, a thorough liar, and so weak-minded as to be capable of turning "monk one day, and a Turk three days after"',[24] was an eccentric whose more innocent activities in-

9 Miniature Hussar costume
used on a lay figure by Arthur Devis
blue satin with pink cuffs and yellow braid
Harris Museum and Art Gallery, Preston

cluded walking round London wearing diamond shoe buckles and a wig made of iron wire. When he travelled in the East in the 1770s, he adopted the customs and dress of the Turks and continued to live like a Turk when living in Venice. His adoption of Turkish dress had the advantage of making his appearance far more dignified and his more unpleasant characteristics are successfully submerged by the authority of the costume. G F Watts said in the nineteenth century: 'As grace of speech is incompatible with slang and vulgar pronunciation, so grace of manner is shorn of its effect by ignoble costume. The dignified reserve of the Eastern potentate or Venetian senator looks like chilling want of sympathy or empty superciliousness in the dress coat and chimney-pot hat.'[25] This argument may be stood on its head. Ill behaviour may be more easily forgotten if the subject removes himself from his true social context by dressing in glamorous foreign dress.

The artist Sir William Allan spent the years from 1805 to 1814 travelling in Russia collecting armour and exotic materials. He returned to Edinburgh bringing these with him to decorate his studio and worked there on a series of paintings celebrating the beauty and romance of the Circassians. Allan worked in his studio wearing a quilted Circassian jacket full of useful little pockets which he filled with paintbrushes; he also etched himself in a suit of chain mail, and William Nicholson painted him as a Circassian (*ill 13*). This example promoted the romantic taste for the Circassians which overtook literature and ordinary women's dress as well as art. Allan seems to have been very willing to lend his costumes out—Geddes painted at least one other portrait of an unnamed person, 'Painted from a dress brought into the country in the possession of Mr W Allan'.[26] It is also possible that the portrait Allan exhibited in the Royal Scottish Academy of 'Lord Castlereagh in the costume of a Circassian Prince, in

11 Edward William Lane (or John Lane) and Mr Lewis in Eastern dress
photograph by David Octavius Hill and Robert Adamson
Scottish National Portrait Gallery

12 Rev Dr John Wilson (1804–1875) in Arab dress
photograph by David Octavius Hill and Robert Adamson
Scottish National Portrait Gallery

which character his lordship appeared at the Bachelors' Fancy Ball given at Edinburgh 1824'[27] showed the sitter in a costume belonging to Allan.

Sir William Allan seems to have enjoyed wearing Circassian dress and he certainly found the jacket full of pockets useful in everyday life. John Zephaniah Bell, uttering the usual diatribe against the drabness of modern dress in 1857, hopefully advocated Circassian dress as not merely beautiful but

13 Sir William Allan (1782–1850) in Circassian dress
by William Nicholson
oil, 91.4 × 71.4 cm
Scottish National Portrait Gallery

practical. 'Some time ago, a gentleman sat to
me for a picture in a dress of Circassia, which
he had worn in that country, and when the
sitting was done he took it off and arrayed
himself in his English costume, and I was
much struck with the difference. In his
Circassian dress, my sitter looked a grand,
striking figure, such as a man should be; but
when he had suited himself to our streets, his
appearance was completely reversed. And, by
the way, the beautiful Circassian coat, which
was of an orange tawny, was not, with all its
beauty, particularly delicate, for it had been
over and over again washed by its wearer in a
river, and hung over the branch of a tree to
dry.'[28]

The nineteenth century saw the growth of
the taste for a kind of Arcadian pin-up—
pictures of attractive young girls called 'A
Moorland Lassie' or 'A Roman Minstrel'. The
foreign peasant dresses, especially, were
brought into play as more colourful and picturesque. Not surprisingly, these turn up constantly at fancy balls, and Samuel Miller
published a whole pamphlet just on *Fishwives'
and Fishgirls' Costumes* in 1883. Sir Charles
Eastlake's portrait of Mrs Bellenden Ker of
1835 (*ill 14*) is a good example of the light
picturesque quality of this sort of picture
adapted to fancy portraiture. Lady Eastlake
commented on the popularity of this fashion:
'in certain portraits of ladies, where the subject permitted, he gratified himself as well as
the fair sitters, by attiring them in a fancy
costume. In this way, Mrs Bellenden Ker
appeared as an Italian Contadina with a
basket of grapes, Miss Bury, with long hair
and a white lily; Miss Johnstone (niece of the
Dowager Countess of Essex), also as an Italian
peasant. These "fancy portraits", as they were
called, were greatly admired, and would have
filled his hands with this class of occupation,
had he not pertinaciously refused to devote
himself to portraiture.'[29]

14 Mrs Charles Bellenden Ker as an Italian peasant
girl
by Sir Charles Eastlake
oil, 75 × 61 cm
Tate Gallery

The Influence of Old Masters

15 Peter, Lord Gwydir (1782–1865) in Vandyckian dress
by Richard Cosway, 1807
pencil and wash, 28 × 21.5 cm
Earl of Ancaster

Naturally enough, one of the major artists who influenced British painters in the eighteenth and nineteenth centuries was Rembrandt, but his influence on portraiture was not as great. Whereas many artists were whole-hearted in their admiration for him, few sitters could be persuaded to allow themselves to be painted in an imitation of Rembrandt's manner. Such portraits as had the reputation of being Rembrandtesque were usually either of eccentrics like Edward Wortley Montagu (*ill 10*) or of artists. A portrait of William Allan in Circassian dress was described by Geddes' wife as 'quite in the manner of Rembrandt and admirably executed'.[30] The reasons for the hostility of sitters were the heavy and unflattering emphasis on dark and light of the imitations and their lack of gentility. Writing in the mid-eighteenth century, George Vertue recorded that Dr Richard Mead, a sophisticated art collector, had been upset by an etching of himself in the manner of Rembrandt done by Arthur Pond 'in short ruff-hair—no wigg &c' and wanted to suppress it 'from whence this proceeded the Dr would not give any answer nor reason one may easily guess, that it appears like an old mumper, as Rhimebrandts heads usually do. Such kind of works will give pleasure to Virtuosi but not to the publick Eye. of the nice part of human nature & modish people'.[31] More than a hundred years later, in 1864, William Bewick expressed a similar view of such a portrait: 'The portrait of T Bewick that I possess was painted by Bell, in the style of Rembrandt, with the hat on, the light falling on one cheek and the side of the nose; and this, with the white neckcloth and frill, is the only light in the picture. It is artistical, but not a domestic picture by any means, and no one would like a family likeness to be so treated.'[32]

By far more sympathetic to the modish people, and even more admired by portrait painters, were the works of Anthony Van Dyck. About 1730 it became fashionable for people to have their portraits painted in Vandyckian dress, or more often in an adaptation of Vandyckian dress to the present fashion. The Duchess of Marlborough wrote to her granddaughter the Duchess of Bedford

16 John, Lord Mountstuart (1744–1814) in Vandyckian dress
by Johann Zoffany
oil, 91.5 × 71 cm
Earl of Harrowby

about a portrait she was commissioning from Isaac Whood: 'I desire that Mr Whood will condescend to copy that picture that was done by Vandyke for that charming Countess of Bedford in the Gallery. The white satin clothes and the posture I would have just the same for you. And I remember particularly that I liked the neck extremely. And I am sure, if he copies that, it will be more like yours than any he will draw for you.' When

her granddaughter expressed her dislike of this incongruous dress, the Duchess of Marlborough explained that asking for a version of a Van Dyck portrait was one way of persuading a mediocre painter to produce a good picture 'whatever dress it is in, the neck may be copied by the Countess of Bedford's, and the hands and arms and the posture of the same, for I cannot fancy that Mr Whood will do so well of his own head as by copying such a Vandyke. And he need not know that I have no opinion of his fancy as to the posture, or giving it a good air in the dress. Most of our best painters now make the limbs tame, and they very seldom make a picture stand well... For all Mr Whood's pictures that I have seen are disagreeable in their postures and dresses. And if you think Vandyke's dress too old-fashioned for this age, he may imitate the Countess of Bedford's as to the white satin and alter the sleeve and waist and make the hair as you like to have it.'[33]

The taste for Vandyckian portraits remained strong for most of the eighteenth century, fostered by drapery painters like Josef Van Haecken and artists like Richard Cosway. Cosway's drawing of Peter, Lord Gwydir (*ill 15*) is probably based on the artist's own invention and is just an elegant piece of affectation. Johann Zoffany's portrait of Lord Mountstuart (*ill 16*) is more likely, to judge by its detail, to be a painting of an actual costume worn for a masquerade. Vandyckian dress was a common masquerade costume in the eighteenth century and elements of it, like the lace collar, were also used in everyday dress from the 1770s.

The admiration of portrait painters for the work of Van Dyck was a constant feature of

21

the two centuries. Sir Joshua Reynolds had reservations about the fashion for Van Dyck portraits when considering such pictures as the one by Isaac Whood: 'By this means it must be acknowledged very ordinary pictures acquired something of the air and effect of the works of Van Dyck, and appeared, therefore, at first sight to be better pictures than they were...'[34] Nevertheless, he acknowledged Van Dyck's supremacy in portraiture, '...the place which Vandyck, all things considered, so justly holds as the first of portrait painters'.[35] A number of Reynolds' own pictures show his sitters in Vandyckian dress and his portrait of Mr Huddesforde and Mr Bampfylde is indebted to Van Dyck also for the general composition and arrangement of the figures (ill 17).

In 1836 Sir David Wilkie expressed a similarly high opinion of his work: 'Vandyke does not, indeed, share in the refined elegance or high science of Raphael, or equal the vivacity and fire of Rubens, nor the startling look of individuality in Velasquez; but there is withal an ease and grace, a silent though living repose, which bring before us the eminent and lovely of his age, as if they had every quality of life save that of movement; yet they seem about to move, having only ceased from moving when we came to look at them. The art of Vandyke is indeed adapted to every capacity: he captivates all beholders by a silent reality, which alike attracts attention and retains it. It may be said of him, that his happy art of portraiture has done more, for one at least of the personages he has painted, than portraiture has done for anyone that ever lived. No one has been ever so rendered by resemblance as Charles I: of this monarch, the portraits by Vandyke are such perfect likenesses, such truly breathing effigies, that they serve to give more of a posthumous existence to man than had ever been bestowed by any human means before...'[36] By the middle of the century, the taste for Van Dyck as the first of the portrait painters was being diluted by a preference for other artists. Lady Elizabeth Eastlake reckoned Vandyckian costume was suitable only for those under fifteen years of age and thought it pretty rather than distinguished. She herself

preferred Reynolds' work: 'To our view the average costume of Sir Joshua was excessively beautiful. We go through a gallery of his portraits with feelings of intense satisfaction that there should have been a race of women who could dress so decorously, so intellectually and withal so becomingly.'[37] Millais' remark about Van Dyck's *Charles I* in check trousers is not an admission of Van Dyck's greater skill in portraiture but a statement of Millais' belief that his portraits would be as good, if not better, if the common dress of the day was as elegant as Van Dyck's. Although artists were no longer quite so whole-hearted in their admiration, Vandyckian and cavalier dress remained very popular at fancy dress parties (ill 18).

The taste of artists for the work of Van Dyck was reinforced by the more general taste for the costume of the period. James Robinson Planché, who wrote the two most authoritative general works on costume of the nineteenth century, said of the Restoration period: 'Taste and elegance were abandoned for extravagance and folly, and the male costume, which in the time of Charles I had reached the highest point of picturesque splendour, degenerated and declined from this moment, and expired in the square coat, cocked hat, full-bottomed wig, and jackboots of the following century.'[38] This opinion was echoed by the Sobieski Stuarts in their work *The Costume of the Clans* of 1845. They attributed a similar decline in the splendour of highland dress to the moral standards of the Restoration, 'but when the Restoration revived the brilliancy of a court from the sordid puritanism of the republic, the last gleam of chivalry which had touched the stately persons of the cavaliers, returned no more in the resurrection of the throne. A new era of licentiousness excited the debasing wantonness of fashion; and from the period when the last of the cavaliers put off the last doublet, the dignity and grandeur of chivalry "declined and degenerated...".'[39] This argument is more remarkable than it at first seems, since it is probable that the cavalier highland magnificence illustrated in *The Costume of the Clans* was a figment of the Sobieski Stuart imagination. The sources they quote for these costumes were not to be found in 1845 and have not been seen since. The Sobieski Stuarts claimed descent from Prince Charles Edward Stuart and, therefore, a right to the British throne. Their interest in Charles I may be explained by Sir Thomas Dick Lauder, who said in a letter to Walter Scott: 'What his [their father's] connection with the Prince may have been, it is difficult to say, but this I know that the elder of the two brothers is so perfectly the *image* of *Charles the first*, that the miraculous likeness strikes everyone who sees him. It is indeed as if one of Vandykes pictures of that monarch had walked out of its frame, and bodied itself forth in tartan.'[40] Through their printed works and their own example, the Sobieski Stuarts undoubtedly had a considerable influence on the highland revival of the nineteenth century. One of the more eccentric examples of this influence is personified by the Scottish nationalist Theodore Napier, who 'habitually

18 Lord Charles Montagu as *Charles I* for the Devonshire House Ball, 1897
photograph from *The Devonshire House Fancy Dress Ball*
National Library of Scotland

19 Theodore Napier (b 1845) in 'cavalier highland dress'
by unknown photographer
Scottish National Portrait Gallery

20 Helena (or Suzanne) Fourment
by Sir Peter Paul Rubens
oil, 186 × 85 cm
Calouste Gulbenkian Foundation, Lisbon

wore the dress of a highland chieftain of the cavalier period' (*ill 19*).

Just as Charles I's court was made more appealing by the elegant art of Van Dyck, so was Van Dyck's painting rendered more interesting by the history of Charles I. This King, like Mary, Queen of Scots, was a subject of deep interest and common discussion in the eighteenth and nineteenth centuries. The romantic resemblance between the two lies mostly in their deaths, both of which could be linked to religious as well as monarchical principle, and they were both also personally attractive figures, Mary because of her reputation, Charles because of the assistance of Van Dyck's art. An example of the popular interest in Charles I appears in Joseph Farington's diary of 1806, which quotes William Wilberforce at dinner in the following remarkable opinion, he 'spoke of the Character of Charles 1st and said His behaviour during his imprisonment, at his trial, and at his death, was so pure, so religious as to be exemplary. It had never perhaps been exceeded.'[41] Such was the interest in the portraits of Charles that A M W Stirling reports the conversation of 1864 between Charles Simon, the surgeon, and George Richmond, the artist, in a general biography published more than sixty years later: 'Thereupon Sir John specially instanced the case of Charles I, whom, he complained, painters had combined to idealize, giving to a face which was weak and shifty a look of intellect that it did not rightfully possess. "A portrait," he pronounced emphatically, "should represent the truth and nothing but the truth."

"Ah," said George Richmond, "but the truth lovingly told."[42]

The survival for nearly two hundred years of the taste for Vandyckian dress is explained by a combination of an uncomplicated visual pleasure with the 'romantic' cavalier interest. More extraordinary than this was the influence of individual paintings on fancy portraits and dress. One of the most important restrictions on the appreciation and imitation of the different styles of dress and painting was simply that until 1824 and the foundation of the National Gallery in London there were

Lady Mary Stewart
Wife to Lord Fortrose.

21 Mary, Countess of Fortrose (d 1751)
by Allan Ramsay, 1749
oil, 127 × 101.5 cm
Raisley Moorsom Esq

22 costume sketch
by Josef Van Haecken
black and white chalk, 39.7 × 35.2 cm
National Gallery of Scotland

26

no publicly owned art galleries. This meant that to view fine works of art a painter had either to tour round asking special permission to see private collections or wait for the rare public exhibitions mounted by private individuals. As a result, the occasional glimpses that artists and amateurs achieved of great works of art had a far greater impact on them.

The most remarkable case of the influence of a single picture on fancy portraiture is the portrait of Helena (or Suzanne) Fourment by Rubens (*ill 20*). In the early eighteenth century, Sir Robert Walpole, the Prime Minister, bought the painting as a Van Dyck and immediately it became the century's most fashionable picture. Endless versions of this painting, adapted more or less to a kind of contemporary dress, appear in portraits from the 1730s to the 1780s, growing less recognisable as the years pass. Artists like Joseph Highmore, Thomas Hudson, Arthur Devis, Allan Ramsay (*ill 21*), and Thomas Gainsborough turned out hundreds of Fourment imitations. An important figure in this industry was the drapery painter Josef Van Haecken, whose drawings of costume contain several Fourment variations (*ills 22, 23*) which he used to dress the sitters of Highmore's, Hudson's, and Ramsay's portraits. A whole series of these paintings provides a very curious effect like a collection of cinematic stills—hands go up and down, the feather fan is raised and dropped, the colours change, little ruffs appear, modest infills appear in the neckline, ankles come and go. By the time of Gainsborough's *Hon Mrs Graham* (*ill 24*) the relationship to the original picture is tenuous in the extreme, resting in the little

23 costume sketch
by Josef Van Haecken
black and white chalk, 46 × 30.3 cm
National Gallery of Scotland

25 fashion plate showing a 'Flemish' dress derived
from the Fourment portrait
from *Petit Courrier des Dames*, 1837
Adam Dickson Esq

24 The Hon Mrs Mary Graham (1757–1792)
by Thomas Gainsborough
oil, 237 × 154 cm
National Gallery of Scotland

26 Mary, Duchess of Ancaster (d 1793)
by J McArdell after Thomas Hudson
mezzotint, 50.5 × 35 cm
Scottish National Portrait Gallery

upturned feathered hat, the string of pearls across the bodice pinned by a brooch, the ribbon-tied sleeves, the feather in the hand, and the looped up overskirt. These details relate more to the idea of the picture by Rubens than to the actual representation.

A later example of a Rubens painting which had a considerable impact in art circles is the painting known as the *Chapeau de Paille*, now in the National Gallery. This was brought over in 1823 and exhibited in

29 Charlotte Nasmyth (1804–1884) as *Summer*
by Andrew Geddes
oil, 81.3 × 64.2 cm
National Gallery of Scotland

28 sketches from Rubens' *Chapeau de Paille* and for *Summer* by Andrew Geddes
pastel, 11.8 × 9 cm and 15.2 × 11.5 cm
National Gallery of Scotland

London where tens of thousands of people paid to see it. Henry Wyatt was among the artists who imitated the picture closely in his portrait of a Mrs Macdougal of the 1830s.[43] Andrew Geddes, who was very impressed by the painting, portrayed Charlotte Nasmyth in an adaptation of the picture which he called *Summer*. This serves as a very good example of the loose derivation from another artist's work since, without the original drawings by Geddes, the association between the pictures would be far from obvious (*ills 28, 29*).

30

Neoclassical Dress

31 William Hamilton of Bangour (1704–1754) as a
classical poet
by Gavin Hamilton
oil, 91.5 × 71.1 cm
Scottish National Portrait Gallery

In the eighteenth and nineteenth centuries, the dependence on classical training as the basis of education and taste had an effect on the arts that has only recently been abandoned. The results of this influence are not always obvious to our own eyes because we have not had this training ourselves and many minor and, indeed, major allusions in art to the classical authorities may pass unnoticed. However, the whole-hearted classical portrait, such as the portrait of Alderman Sawbridge by Benjamin West, is clearly wrong in its period and stands out from the general run (*ill 30*). The classicised painted portrait was far less common than the classical sculptured portrait. The reasons for this are two-fold: firstly, that the great portrait sculpture of the classical age had survived as an example and, secondly, that sculpture was reckoned to be a more public art than painting (as well as being more expensive) and, therefore, required the greater dignity which Greece and Rome were thought to have. Sir Joshua Reynolds expressed this in his *Discourses delivered to the students of the Royal Academy* in 1769:

'As Greece and Rome are the foundations from whence have flowed all kinds of excellence, to that veneration which they have a right to claim for the pleasure and knowledge which they have afforded us, we voluntarily add our approbation of every ornament and every custom that belonged to them, even to the fashion of their dress. For it may be observed that, not satisfied with them in their own place, we make no difficulty of dressing statues of modern heroes or senators in the fashion of Roman armour or peaceful robe; we go so far as to hardly bear a statue in any other drapery.

The figures of the great men of those nations have come down to us in sculpture. In sculpture remain almost all the excellent specimens of ancient art. We have so far associated personal dignity to the persons thus represented, and the truth of art to their manner of representation, that it is not in our power any longer to separate them. This is not so in painting; because having no excellent ancient portraits, that connection was never formed. Indeed we could no more

venture to paint a general officer in a Roman military habit than we could make a statue in the present uniform.'[44] This statement is, of course, an exaggeration on Reynolds' part—there are plenty of eighteenth-century statues in eighteenth-century dress and a substantial number of eighteenth-century portraits in classical dress—but as a bias of taste the argument stands.

One of the reasons for portraits in classical dress is, as Reynolds says, the increased dignity given to the sitter. The person and actions of the sitter became associated with the weight and authority of the classical age. The words and deeds of the great classical orators and politicians were esteemed so much more highly than those of contemporaries that to dress a statue, or more rarely a painted portrait, in a toga was not merely a compliment of a high order but took him out of his age and made him a timeless authority. The same idea prompted the portraits of eighteenth-century soldiers in classical armour, who thus became associated with the great generals of antiquity. Likewise, the portrait of the poet William Hamilton by Gavin Hamilton takes him out of his true eighteenth-century context and ranges him with the great classical poets (*ill 31*).

This reasoning spreads yet further and beyond dignity alone into a large range of characters and virtues. Statuary, paintings, and engravings, even when the central portrait was in contemporary dress, were frequently decorated with classical figures demonstrating the virtues of the subject. The personification or embodiment of individual human abilities and characteristics was an undisputed classical province and the classical gods remained alongside these personifications as a form of metaphor current in poetry and art: the eighteenth century inherited rules for painting, for example, war as Mars, chastity or hunting as Diana, love as Cupid. This elementary and familiar system of symbolism was extremely useful to artists, as it was to poets, as a short cut to flattery. Dress a woman's son as Cupid, place him on her knee, and she becomes Venus, Goddess of Love; paint an eagle beside her and place a cup in her hand and she is Hebe, carried off by Jupiter for her exceptional beauty. This kind of portrait was so popular in the late eighteenth century that the sister of Ann Forbes, a mediocre portrait painter trying to make a living in London, wrote home complaining: 'but the Taste of the present times

32 unknown lady as a sorceress
by Richard Cosway, 1805
pencil and wash, 36.8 × 28.9 cm
Duke of Hamilton

here is confounding Portrait and History Painting together, which is a thing Peculiar to Britain, amongst all the Paintings we saw both in France & Italy they were kept perfectly [?] but here the Misses are not pleased without they be Flying in the Air, or Riding on a cloud feeding Jupiter's Eagle.'[45]

Richard Cosway, who was an enthusiast for such portraits, was adept at this kind of flattery. His drawing of a young lady (*ill 32*),

33 Lady Emily Kerr as a bacchante
by William Hoare
oil, 177 × 146 cm
Holburne of Menstrie Museum, Bath

who is lightly disguised as a classical sorceress, reads as a static poem which shows her stepping into a cabalistic circle with aromatic herbs burning on an elaborate brazier sending up aphrodisiac clouds with Cupid perched on top, summoned by her wand to pour a love potion into the cup she is holding. Unfortunately, we do not know who the subject of this portrait was but she serves as an example of the remarkable lack of modesty in displaying attainments or charms which the classical metaphor made respectable. Equally striking in this way is the portrait of Lady Emily Kerr (*ill 33*), a very young girl, whose parents presumably ordered the extremely large painting of her as a bacchante without considering that it in any way associated her with wild and drunken bacchanalian orgies. Possibly classical orgies had a respectable antique gloss. Miss Forbes' complaints at least make it clear that the taste for these symbolic portraits was common to both sitter and artist and that they were not foisted on an unwilling or innocent public by the painters.

In effect, what these portraits were aiming at was a synthesis or compromise between history and portrait painting. In the later eighteenth and early nineteenth century the major portrait painters yearned to be freed from the drudgery of endless face painting and to be allowed to express themselves in ideal compositions and forms rather than accurate copying of dull faces and finicky tailoring. The corsetted and restricting clothes that were worn by women, particularly, for most of the eighteenth and nineteenth centuries dictated a stiffness of pose and movement that was not just a question of manners or convention. The straight back and neck and the hard form of the eighteenth- and nineteenth-century lady were created as much by her clothes as by her training. The woman wearing a corset could not recline easily like the lady in the Liberty advertisement (*ill 34*). A portrait painter interested in painting a standard portrait showing a woman in her customary dress was thus limited not merely by the lines and colour of the dress but also by the effect of the dress on the woman. In, for example, the exaggerated wide panier skirts or tall wigs of the 1760s, or the extremely tight toothpaste tube dresses of the 1870s, a woman was severely restricted in the speed and range of movements she could risk without making herself ridiculous. She could drift, glide, or tiptoe but attempts to run, leap, or throw her arms in the air would, for most of the eighteenth and nineteenth centuries, have been accompanied by rending material or twanging whalebone or, at the least, have achieved a highly ludicrous effect. Our idealised view of the past is apt to persuade us that the eighteenth and nineteenth centuries were possessed of an elegance and grace that our brash modern age has lost but it was a vulnerable and highly studied elegance, by no means as universal as the paintings of the time would have us believe.

The most striking features of the classical portraits of women are the display of the shape of the body and the figure in movement. In most contemporary dress, the body was not to be seen in its natural lines. The

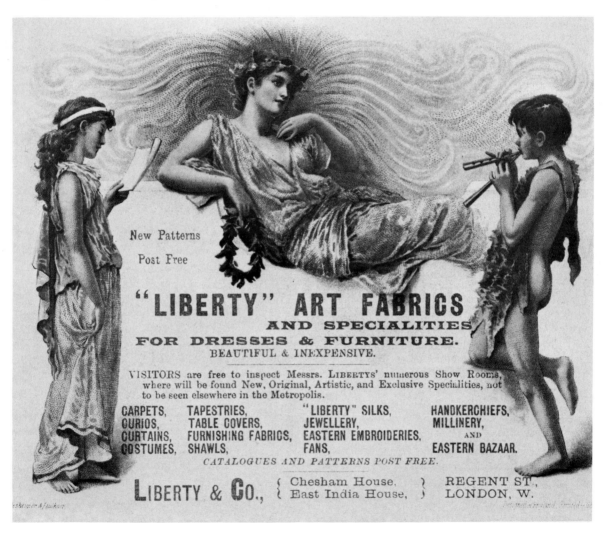

34 advertisement for Liberty & Co
back cover of Savoy theatre programme, 6 July 1889
Theatre Museum, Victoria and Albert Museum

35 *Form versus Fashion*, satire on modern dress with the ghost of Galatea reacting to fashionable dress
by Gourlay Steell junior, 1885
watercolour and pencil, 35.2 × 25.4 cm
Scottish National Portrait Gallery

36 Princess Amelia (1783–1810)
by Peter Edward Stroehling, 1807
oil, 57.1 × 41.6 cm
reproduced by gracious permission of Her Majesty The Queen

occasional exceptions come with the neoclassical fashions of the turn of the eighteenth century and the aesthetic movement of the late nineteenth century which were, significantly, both periods heavily influenced by classicism and by art. The beauty of the female form, especially, which is a subject that has not unnaturally obsessed male artists since art began, was largely denied to portrait painters. The wholesale employment of drapery painters by the portraitists of the eighteenth century is in itself an indication of the pre-eminence of the clothes over the body—the portraitist painted the head and hands and the rest was just 'drapery'. Joshua Reynolds, arguing against the exact representation of modern dress, made the point that the clothes were not a part of the man or his essential nature: '...after a time, the dress is only an amusement for an antiquarian; and if it obstructs the general design of the piece, it is to be disregarded by the artist. Common sense must here give way to a higher sense. In the naked form and in the disposition of the drapery, the difference between one artist and another, is principally seen. But if he is compelled to exhibit the modern dress, the naked form is entirely hid and the drapery is already disposed by the skill of the tailor. Were a Phidias to obey such commands, he would please no more than an ordinary sculptor; since in the inferior parts of every art, the learned and the ignorant are nearly upon a level.'[46]

The classical portrait had the advantage of bringing back the body as an essential and prominent part of the sitter's attractions (*ill 36*). With the loose and simple classical drapery, moreover, the range of poses and movement was far greater than in an ordinary portrait. None of the full-length portraits of women in this section would have looked right to contemporary eyes if they had not been wearing classical dress. Even Lady Charlotte Campbell (*colour plate 1*), who at first sight is sitting in a relatively simple pose, would have seemed inappropriate if she were wearing a stiffer, more formal dress, when her right leg would have had to be brought further forward to balance the composition. It is significant that Tischbein, who was not

primarily a portrait painter, wished to paint Lady Charlotte not exclusively for her highly classical features but because he saw and admired her in swift movement, which was uncommon in a young lady at that period. 'The Duke of Argyll was also approaching, his daughter on his arm, when a coach was suddenly seen to be driving straight at them. The daughter was terrified, and leaving her father's arm, fled to save herself. Wherever she ran, another coach came towards her at full tilt. She turned again, hurried out of the path of one, but having fled into a clear space, yet more coaches drove towards her. Thus she fled in terror from one spot to another, in and out of the dashing coaches. Quite apart from the sympathy that one felt for her, since she believed herself to be in danger of her life, it offered a splendid sight to one with eyes for the swift and strenuous active motion of a beautiful figure. One sees lovely movements in certain dances, but what is that compared to this natural running, twisting, and turning, alternately decisive and indecisive. Every movement was expressive and clearly showed her inner emotion, as well as her slender, youthful form, since her dress clung close about her through the pressure of the air, through which she was, so to speak, fleeing. What I had formerly only admired in Art, the lovely, youthful, fleeing figures on bas-reliefs and the swaying dancers of the paintings at Herculaneum, I now saw here in Nature itself. No planned intention could have brought to execution so skilfully what was being done here by chance. Everything was playing its part, the time and place, especially the green glades of the forest, where I had seen the nimble stags and does running and the huntsmen on their horses. As in special entertainments which are meant to make a deep impression, the most delightful thing is saved up until the end, so I could see all that had gone before as just such a preparation for what was now offered to my eyes. This exquisite, slender, boyish figure fleeing like a frightened deer running through the trees. Thus Aurora drifts before the chariot of Apollo! A few days later I painted her in a wood, a scroll of music on her lap, with her arm raised to bend down a branch, enticing a deer to feed from its leaves.'[47]

The classicised portrait and the taste for classical dress were not necessarily a slavish attempt to copy the antique. Quite often, what the artists and admirers of the mode were interested in was a wider concept—that of nature or simplicity. Joshua Reynolds, who considered the matter at some length, believed that his period had too many inbuilt, if not warped, prejudices in favour of incorrect taste that made it difficult to recognise simplicity and nature without assistance. This assistance would come most effectively from a study of the antique. 'Here then, as before, we must have recourse to the Ancients as instructors. It is from a careful study of their works that you will be enabled to attain to the real simplicity of Nature; they will suggest many observations which would probably escape you, if your study were confined to Nature alone. And, indeed, I cannot help suspecting, that in this instance the ancients had an easier task than the Moderns. They had, probably, little or nothing to unlearn, as their manners were nearly approaching to this desirable simplicity; while the modern Artist, before he can see the truth of things, is obliged to remove a veil with which the fashion of the times has thought proper to cover her.'[48] Reynolds' use of the classical ideal in portraits was not intended to reproduce the classical examples but to abstract from them a simplicity of form and movement. Frederick, Lord Leighton, who was not a portrait painter, expressed a similar idea a hundred years later in 1873: 'By degrees, however, my growing love for Form made me intolerant of the restraint and exigencies of costume, and led me more and more, and finally to a class of subjects, or, more accurately to a set of conditions, in which supreme scope is left to pure artistic qualities, in which no form is imposed upon the artist by the tailor, but in which every form is made obedient to the conception of the design he has in hand. These conditions classic subjects afford, and as vehicles, therefore of abstract form, which is a thing not of one time but of all time, these subjects can never be obsolete, and though to many they are a dead letter, they can never be an anachronism.'[49]

This taste for simplicity most commonly expressed itself, in portraiture, in a form that was not strictly fancy dress so much as the evasion of dress. By the use of a piece of vague drapery that might pass for a cloak, part or all of the everyday dress could be covered and an effect closer to the desired simplicity could be achieved. David Wilkie described this in a work by Thorwaldsen in 1826: 'His statue of Prince Poniatowski in marble is a work of a high class, showing in what way the costume of a modern general may be evaded, by representing him in drapery best suited to sculpture by being adapted to no particular time; a method of generalizing common to the ancients themselves, as exemplified in the Roman equestrian bronze of Marcus Aurelius, and by the Greek marble figure of Demosthenes.'[50]

The period of actual dress most obviously influenced by classical taste is, of course, the late eighteenth and early nineteenth century when theoretical and artistic taste spread to affect practical taste. Enthusiasts like Sir William Hamilton or Thomas Hope dressed their wives in the Greek fashion. Mrs Hope's 'Grecian' dress (*ill 37*) loosely derives from Thomas Hope's *The Costume of the Ancients* which he published in 1809 primarily for the use of artists. He later published a book, specifically to influence modern dress, called *Designs of Modern Costume*. Men were almost totally resistant to the lure of classical dress— a bid to adopt classical togas in revolutionary France alas failed—the so-called 'neoclassical' socks (which to my eye may as easily be Saxon socks) seem to be a solitary and inexplicable aberration (*ill 38*). The sole male concession to the neoclassical fashion was to wear the hair short and casually curled 'à la Titus' or 'à la Brutus'. Women's fashion went much further. The high waistline, the narrow dress with the wide hoop removed, which could reveal the shape of the body beneath more readily, the bordered material and the hair bound up with a fillet were all employed separately or together. Occasionally, this resulted in an effect that is almost classical. But a wholesale adoption of the fashion of another place or time is most unlikely. The nineteenth-century desire for classicised dress

37 The Hon Mrs Thomas Hope in a 'Grecian' dress
after George Dawe
mezzotint, 59.7 × 38.1 cm
Scottish National Portrait Gallery

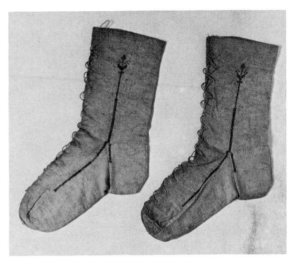

38 'neoclassical' man's socks
buff cotton, early nineteenth century
Strangers' Hall, Norwich

is commonly tempered as in the following attack made by Lady Charlotte Campbell on French dress in 1814, when it is still neoclassical to our eyes in so far as it still adheres to the high waistline and narrower skirt: 'To my idea, the more nearly women's dress assimilates to the antique, the more beautiful. Our climate and manners always demand some difference, but at present the French discard all resemblance to what one has been taught to think beautiful, time immemorial.'[51]

In practice, what came most effectively between neoclassical revival and modern dress was not a sensible consideration of climate and manners but fashion and the dressmaker. Fashion never has and never will aim to clothe us in the most practical and beautiful way possible. It is an art form of its own willing to borrow ideas and decorate its own conceptions but no more prepared to copy the antique slavishly than the artists of the same time. Elements of the 'neoclassical' dress at the beginning of the nineteenth century agree with the classical age (*ills 39, 40*) but the close-fitting bodices, tight sleeves, and lack of fulness in the folds, and indeed the inability to stick to the classical idea that led to Turkish turbans, Polonese skirts, ruffs, Tudor sleeves amongst many discordant features and accessories, turned the revival back into fashion. The same thing happened during the period of aesthetic interest in dress at the end of the century: a taste for classicism and diluted mediaevalism received via the paintings of Burne-Jones and Rossetti failed to win over the fashion of the time. The example of the 'classical' dress of 1890 starts with a ruff at the neck and makes a passable attempt at a Greek fold from the shoulders but underneath it is still the same heavily corsetted 1890s shape (*ill 41*). The historical confusion of the 'artistic' dress produced by Liberty's was certainly deliberate. The *Black and White* magazine of May 1891 describes one of their

39 'neoclassical' fashion plate
from *Costume Parisien*, 1798
Adam Dickson Esq

40 'neoclassical' fashion plate
from *Costume Parisien*, 1803
Adam Dickson Esq

dresses in the following terms: 'Since it is to Messrs Liberty that we owe the so-called art fabrics—the very term suggesting the materials for sartorial pictures or poems in drapery—one has only to enter their charmingly decorated rooms to find oneself surrounded by works of art in embryo, inspirations for the pictorial harmonies of a Leighton or an Alma Tadema, or for the scenic symphonies of a W S Gilbert.

For instance, where is the painter who

41 dress by Liberty Costumes *c* 1890, traditionally a wedding dress
white silk
Birmingham City Museum

42 dress by Marius Fortuny, early twentieth century
pale olive-green, mushroom-pleated silk
Royal Scottish Museum

THIS PAGAN HEALTH.

*Why is it that, in symbolising
healthy nerves, we can find no
finer examples than the real
and mythical figures of pagan
days? How seldom to-day,
in office or shop, train or street,
does one see a man or woman
exuberant with nervous energy.*

43 advertisement for Sanatogen
from *Illustrated London News*, 19 November 1938

44 advertisement for Cramp's patent stocking
suspenders
from Marie Schild, *Album of Fancy Costumes*, 1885

would not find inspiration in such a gown as this [illustration], with its artistic combination of olive green velveteen with a maize-coloured silk gauze? The graceful train which falls from the shoulder resembles the form of an old Roman mantle, while the dress, with an embroidered belt under the arms confining the folds of the drapery, makes for the mediaeval, and this composite garment is fashioned into a perfectly harmonious whole. Thus do Messrs Liberty scientifically graft a feature of the fashion of one period on to another, and so compose a new style, just as the enterprising horticulturalist grafts one chrysanthemum on to another to produce a splendid new flower.'

Of the dresses we illustrate here, the most convincingly classical and the least like a grafted chrysanthemum is undoubtedly the dress by Marius Fortuny (*ill 42*). This dates from the early twentieth century, when the deliberate interest in the reform of dress in a classical direction had died down. The dress is an example of individual classical influence on one designer and was inspired by the statue of the charioteer at Delphi.

The later nineteenth-century dress reformers and aesthetes were interested in classical dress not just for the flowing lines but for the freedom of movement. The looseness and lack of constriction inherent in classical dress recommended it to those concerned with physical health and the Greek interest in athletics made the connection academically respectable. In 1880, Dr George Wilson was one of many who hopefully advocated the reform of dress in this direction: 'On physiological grounds, the classic mode was incomparably superior to the modern style of dress, because the whole weight of the garments was borne by the shoulders, and not from a waist constricted by strings and bands, if not by tight-laced stays. It may be true that the style of garments worn by Greek and Roman women may not be suited to our colder climate, but the closer the adaptation of modern apparel is to that style, so much the more artistic taste will be displayed, and the better will be the health enjoyed.'[52] The association of loose classical dress with greater health was not surprising in view of the serious distortion and constriction caused by corsets especially. A

curious offshoot of this association was an advertising convention that antiquity equalled health, which lasted well into the twentieth century with the Sanatogen advertisements of the 1930s (*ill 43*) and spawned on the way such oddities as the small child skipping about wearing a classical tunic with Cramp's patent sock suspenders (*ill 44*).

The interest of this period in health and exercise, which in itself required new, looser clothes, finally brought the ideals of classicism into this area. George Du Maurier, who satirised the elegant aesthetic droop which was ultimately derived from classical grace, also satirised the association of classicism with tennis in several cartoons. One of these is illustrated here (*ill 45*). Another, which shows a girl admiring a young man playing tennis who looks like a Greek god and proves a sore disappointment in city suiting, has a moral: 'Why not wear White Flannel Shirts and Knickerbockers every day, even in the City, and look like Olympian Gods (since it seems they used to dress something like that), all the year round?'. Neoclassicism had come a long way to be reduced to the absurdities of patent suspenders and tennis.

MODERN ÆSTHETICS.

Materfamilias. " WHERE HAVE YOU BEEN ALL THE MORNING, GIRLS?"   *Sophronia Cassandra.* " WE'VE BEEN PRACTISING OLD GREEK ATTITUDES AT LAWN-TENNIS, MAMMA?"
Papa (who is not æsthetic). " AH! HOPE YOU LIKE IT, I'M SURE!"   *Sophronia Cassandra.* " VERY MUCH, PAPA—ONLY WE *NEVER HIT THE BALL!*"

45 satire on neoclassical athletics
by George Du Maurier
from *Punch,* 1878

Tableaux, Attitudes & Photography

One of the most extraordinary art forms which reached its height of popularity in the nineteenth century was the *tableau vivant*, an imitation by people of a painting. William Bewick, who took part in one at Lady Westmoreland's house in Rome in 1827, described the occasion in a letter: 'During the evening there will be exhibited what are called *tableaux*, which are no more than people dressed up to represent the different characters in some celebrated picture. They are placed behind a gold frame in the positions and with the expressions of the picture. A green cloth is put all round the frame, and hides the light or anybody that may be behind. Then a piece of thin black gauze is thrown over the front of the frame, and the effect is perfectly beautiful. There are several of these pictures made during the evening, in which the noblemen and ladies, and people of fashion, stand for the characters; I mean such as have faces and figures adapted for it. The character that I have to take has been twice rehearsed. The subject is a young warrior, dressed in steel armour, and his page is buckling on his shoulder-piece. A young lady of exquisite beauty is to be the page. Her lovely face and delicate hands will be set off to great advantage by my grim visage, for I am to frown most abominably. Lady Westmoreland calls out, "Frown, Mr Bewick! frown, Sir! You must look cross for once, for this is your page only—you must not think she is a pretty girl."

This is the first piece that has been tried, and those who were placed as judges exclaimed, "Beautiful! Wonderful effect!" and so on. One gentleman, a sculptor, not thinking at the time how it was produced, called out, "How wonderfully like nature!" Another, a painter, came very close with his friend, and, not knowing that the lady was an Englishwoman and understood their conversation, said, "How very like flesh her face is!" and then thinking she was an Italian added, "A devilish pretty girl that page is!" While we were standing so, my page whispered that she should not be able to stand still or keep from laughing if those people were to talk, so I gave the signal and the folding doors were closed.'[53]

47 sketch for a tableau from *Waverley*
by Sir David Wilkie
pen and wash, 19 × 25.8 cm
Marquis of Salisbury

While I can just understand the performers being prepared to equip themselves with elaborate clothes, gold frames, and black gauze as fake varnish just to freeze for a few minutes like a picture while their friends declared how handsome and attractive the effect was, I cannot fathom why the audiences took it so seriously. A tableau is at best a piece of ephemeral cleverness, yet for more than a century artists, royalty, and charity fête organisers expected and apparently received loud applause and enthusiasm for presenting them. It would be less surprising if, for instance, amateur and incompetent artists found in tableaux an easy way of achieving an effect, but throughout the nineteenth century artists of standing were involved in devising and setting them up. This, to me, seems like finding a major sculptor indulging in poker work.

David Wilkie, who was one of the most influential artists of his period, was one of the major figures who performed and popularised tableaux among the British in Rome and in Britain. He discovered the idea in Dresden in 1826: 'I have been much interested by an exhibition at one of their little Theatres, of what they call a Tableau. The curtain is drawn up between the acts, the stage darkened, and at the back is a scene resembling a picture frame, in the interior of which most brilliantly lighted from behind, men and women are arranged in appropriate dresses, to make up the composition of some known picture. One I saw the other night was an interior, after D Teniers. It was the most beautiful reality I ever saw. Mr Chadd, the British minister, was with me. We were quite delighted with it; but so evanescent is the group, that the curtain drops in twenty seconds the people being unable to remain for any longer period in one precise position.'[54] Wilkie was a very laborious artist, constantly drawing, re-drawing, and re-grouping his paintings, so it is probable that he was attracted by the easy effects of the tableau. His name became so closely associated with *tableaux vivants* that satirical political cartoons, such as one by 'H B' (Richard Doyle) of 1832 called *Un Tableau Vivant* and consisting of a take-off of Wilkie's painting of Calabrian

minstrels playing to the Madonna could expect such a reference to be generally understood. Wilkie found himself, as a result, practically loaned out by the Duke of Wellington to the Marchioness of Salisbury, who wanted him not merely to sketch suitable groups for a set of tableaux after Walter Scott, but to attend the rehearsals and organise the figures. He wrote to Sir William Knighton in the royal household, because he was engaged at the time in painting the Queen: 'I am at present in a difficulty in which I must seek your advice. The Duke of Wellington about six weeks ago requested me to assist at the *tableaux* proposed by the Marchioness of Salisbury, to be made in the ensuing week at Hatfield, since which I have been in communication with her Ladyship, and have been making drawings (all from Sir Walter Scott's novels) of her arrangements of the figures, expecting that my labours here would be over in time. Now, as this is not the case, and I am expected as an *assistant* at Hatfield, and have been consulted here by several ladies who are to appear in the tableaux, do you think I might ask for leave of absence from Her Majesty, and for leave to resume my work here afterwards?'[55]

The tableaux Wilkie was concerned with took place in January 1833 at Hatfield and were performed on a grand and deliberate scale, planned at least six weeks in advance and involving not just Wilkie's sketches of the groups but a more detailed and naïve series of costume paintings of the individual figures, though these may have been done after the event. The evening involved a ball and a dinner party and the press was present. The report of one evening paper quoted in *The Times* is so lacking in enthusiasm that the writer must have been there as opposed to merely copying a press release.

'FÊTE AT HATFIELD HOUSE

This fête was remarkable for the "tableaux" exhibited by part of the company, attired in the perfect costume of the times and of the parties they represented. The company consisted of a select party, all in fancy dress, which rendered the scene very striking when

46 sketch for a tableau, presumably from *The Abbot*
by Sir David Wilkie, 1833
pen and wash, 19.8 × 26 cm
Marquis of Salisbury

the *coup d'oeuil* was taken of the whole in that splendid mansion... Amongst the tableaux one of the most remarkable was that taken from the description in *Ivanhoe*, where Rebecca, to avoid the pursuit of the knight, threatens to throw herself from the battlements of the castle. Lady Lyndhurst, covered with jewels, and looking remarkably well, personated Rebecca, and Lord Grimston the Knight; their attitudes, however, were more for effect than according to nature, and Rebecca, instead of looking at the knight when she is supposed to exclaim "That if he advanced a step further she would throw herself headlong from the embrasure", seemed to look quite another way. Whether Wilkie, who placed the parties, is to blame for this, is more than we can say...

The Marchioness of Salisbury, as Lady Edith, was dressed in her favourite carnation-colour silk velvet robe, richly ornamented with jewels and pearls. Lady Sandwich's dress was the subject of general admiration: her Ladyship's bodice was thickly studded with costly brilliants. The Ladies Mildred and Blanche Cecil (the young daughters of the host and hostess) were attired as heralds, and formed an interesting portion of the procession. There were about 700 persons present... [The dresses of the personages who figured in the *tableaux* were magnificent; but no sense but the *sight* was gratified at this *fête*. The niggardly supply of refreshments—there being nothing to eat or drink after the small allowance of tea and hot water was exhausted—made everybody discontended.]'[56]

One of the remarkable features of the Hatfield tableaux, apart from the abundance of jewellery and the weakness of the tea, is that Wilkie was expected to invent the pictures. Tableaux had come to popularity on the back of the Old Masters—the early descriptions of tableaux are clearly derived from the most respectable and famous sources—Titian, Van Dyck and Giorgione, amongst others. But now tableaux had developed from a reproductive into an original art form. Wilkie's drawings for the Hatfield tableaux, with the exception of the one drawing, probably of a scene from *The Abbot*, which shows the group set

within the framework of the columns of Hatfield's Long Gallery where the tableaux were staged (*ill 46*), are indistinguishable from sketches for oil paintings (*ill 47*). Throughout the nineteenth century, professional and amateur artists treated the tableau as a form of artistic expression requiring almost as serious an approach as did paintings. Presidents of the Royal Academy, artists of the social standing of Frederic Leighton and J E Millais were called in to provide designs for tableaux and the subjects chosen by the amateurs read like a list of paintings exhibited at the Royal Academy.

During the visit of the Prince and Princess of Wales to Mar Lodge in 1863, tableaux were arranged by the Hon Lewis Wingfield and Mr Victor Prout. The volume commemorating the visit is largely given over to photographs of the tableaux: Mary, Queen of Scots at Wemyss Castle; Mary, Queen of Scots attended by Rizzio (*ill 48*); Elaine; The Soldier's Return; Charlotte Corday contemplating her picture before her execution; and Faith, Hope and Charity. This list encompasses the greater part of the common artistic range of subjects employed by artists of the period: Romantic Historical, Romantic Literary, Rustic Genre, Moral Historical, and Symbolic. The tableaux 'delighted all who witnessed them by their dramatic vigour and poetic sentiment. Applause of the warmest kind, in which the Prince and Princess heartily joined, repeatedly rewarded the efforts of the performers', according to the text of the volume produced by Mr Prout. However we may doubt this warmness, the fact remains that the Earl and Countess of Fife considered that *tableaux vivants* provided a suitably impressive entertainment for royalty.

In this belief they were not at fault. The young royal family were encouraged by their parents to indulge in dressing up of all kinds, not least in *tableaux vivants*. It is highly significant that one of the entertainments Victoria was first persuaded to enjoy in her melancholy widowed retirement was a series of tableaux staged at Osborne in 1888. These used elaborate theatrical costumes, supplied by Nathan's, with the members of the royal family and household looking more or less

48 *Mary, Queen of Scots attended by Rizzio*
tableau with the Hon Lewis Wingfield and Miss G
Moncrieffe
photograph by Victor Albert Prout, 1863
Scottish National Portrait Gallery

convincing depending on the subject, more convincing in a frozen classical group called 'Homage to Queen Victoria' (*ill 49*), totally unconvincing in a dead pan representation of a riotous dancing scene from *Carmen* (*ill 50*). This last, a surprising choice of subject to perform before Queen Victoria, is an example of the growing theatrical influence on tableaux. Having originated as imitations of paintings in the eighteenth-century theatre, they had finally returned to the theatre for inspiration for pictures. The Victorian theatre had, in fact, for some time specialised in spectacular set-pieces which they called *tableaux vivants*, to display the increasingly elaborate costumes and stage settings as massive three-dimensional pictures.

The royal tableaux, stage-managed by the Hon Alexander Yorke, are fine examples of the increasing elaboration and accuracy required of tableaux. Photographs of later performances show painted backdrops as well as

49 *Homage to Queen Victoria*
tableau with the ladies of Queen Victoria's household at Osborne, 1888
photograph by Byrne and Co
reproduced by gracious permission of Her Majesty The Queen

50 *Carmen*
tableau with Major Bigge, Prince Henry of
Battenberg as Escamillo and Miss Minnie Cochrane
as Carmen, at Osborne, 1888
photograph by Byrne and Co
*reproduced by gracious permission of Her Majesty The
Queen*

stage properties, imported woodland, stuffed tigers, weapons, etc. At least one, the tableau of Bonnie Prince Charlie in hiding (*ill 51*), had background music in the form of the Skye Boat Song.[57] Queen Victoria, pleased by the Osborne performance, casually asked the Hon Alexander Yorke to do it again in 1890 at Balmoral, giving him only three days' warning. In a panic he wrote to Nathan's in London, including a list with measurements of fourteen costumes required:

'Monday, 5th June, Mr. Nathan, the Queen has ordered me to arrange some Tableaux quite in an impromptu way for *Thursday* next which leaves me but little time. So I must ask you to send me out of stock a box of things to help me. They must be at Buckingham Palace to go by messenger on Wednesday 7th inst by 12.30, as the messenger leaves about one o'clock every day for Balmoral. Also send me a black gauze 12-ft by 10-ft and a complete man's dress of a Roumanian or Montenegrin

51 *Charles Edward*
tableau with Princess Victoria of Wales as Flora Macdonald and Prince Albert Victor as Prince Charles Edward, at Balmoral, 1888
photograph by George Washington Wilson
reproduced by gracious permission of Her Majesty The Queen

type for a tableaux, etc etc. In haste to catch the messenger,

Faithfully Yours,
Alexander Yorke.'[58]

Not surprisingly, the results on this occasion were uninspired and only Lord William Cecil, as a pantomime fairy prince raising the Sleeping Beauty, had any success (*ill 52*).

In the late eighteenth century, a similar phenomenon to tableaux arose in the form of the 'attitudes' of Emma Hamilton. Lady Hamilton, the mistress and later the wife of Sir William Hamilton, the British Ambassador in Naples and an enthusiastic collector of antiquities, seems to have been in his eyes a part of her husband's collection. Her attitudes were, in effect, an imitation of classical sculptures and vase figures. Unlike the performers of *tableaux vivants*, she used the minimum of props and a very simple dress. She also had the advantage of having been trained as a

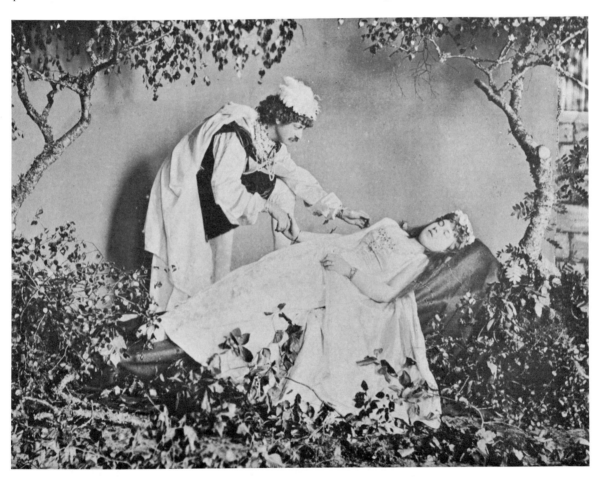

52 *The Sleeping Beauty*
tableau with Princess Alexandra of Edinburgh and
Lord William Cecil, at Balmoral, 1890
by unknown photographer
reproduced by gracious permission of Her Majesty The Queen

53

model, probably posing in Dr Graham's dubious Temple of Health and certainly posing extensively for George Romney, who took a close interest in the theatre. Emma was able to manipulate shawls and draperies with considerable grace and to produce at will a large number and range of expressions. Sir William took an immense and sometimes doubtful pleasure in this skill of Emma's, as in the following account in a letter from her written in 1787: '...they have all got it in their heads I am like the virgin & the[y] do come to beg favours of me. Last night their was two preists came to our house & Sir William made me put the shawl over my head & the preist burst in to tears & kist my feet & said God had sent me a purpose...'[59]

Sir William, however, was not alone in admiring Lady Hamilton's attitudes. They were universally admired. Goethe's *Italian Journey*, for example, speaks very highly of her charms. 'He [Sir William] has had a Greek costume made for her which becomes her extremely. Dressed in this, she lets down her hair and, with a few shawls, gives so much variety to her poses, gestures, expressions, etc, that the spectator can hardly believe his eyes. He sees what thousands of artists would have liked to express realized before him in movements and surprising transformations— standing, kneeling, sitting, reclining, serious, sad, playful, ecstatic, contrite, alluring, threatening, anxious, one pose follows another without a break. She knows how to arrange the folds of her veil to match each mood, and has a hundred ways of turning it into a headdress. The old knight idolizes her and is enthusiastic about everything she does. In her, he has found all the antiquities, all the profiles of Sicilian coins, even the Apollo Belvedere. This much is certain: as a performance it's like nothing you ever saw before in your life.'[60]

Emma Hamilton was a very beautiful woman and it might be thought that the men who describe her so enthusiastically were prejudiced by this fact in favour of her attitudes. Some undoubtedly were: the Count d'Eschpinal described her dancing the fandango: 'Mrs Hart endowed it with a degree of grace and voluptuousness that would have set

53 Emma, Lady Hamilton (?1761–1815)
by Richard Cosway
pencil and watercolour, 22.3 × 14 cm
National Portrait Gallery, London

54

56

55

any man's senses aflame, however cold and insusceptible he might be... Apparently it was to please her benefactor, who is a great lover of art and the antique, that Mrs Hart cultivated her gift of posing in various attitudes. Without seeing her no one could conceive the illusion produced by this beautiful woman for our delight. Were I Sir William Hamilton, I should pass in review all the goddesses of Olympus; I should frequently see Hebe, Venus and the Graces, and sometimes Juno, but rarely Minerva. Sometimes to vary my pleasure, I should look into a luxurious boudoir to see Cleopatra—passionate, tender, amorous—receiving Mark Antony; and sometimes, in a bower of foliage, I should find Alcibiades dallying with Glycera.'[61] No-one could accuse the Count of being a disinterested lover of pure classical art. But her imitations of classical sculpture were also given praise by people who disliked her and thought her socially uncouth. The Comtesse de Boigne, who considered Emma 'a bad woman' and thought she had a 'low mind', was much impressed by her performances and even took part in them occasionally. 'I have sometimes acted with her as a subordinate figure to form a group. She used to place me in the proper position, and arrange my draperies before raising her shawl, which served as a curtain enveloping us both. My fair hair contrasted with her magnificent black hair, to which many of her effects were due.

One day she placed me on my knees before an urn, with my hands together, in an attitude of prayer. Leaning over me, she seemed lost in grief, and both of us had our hair dishevelled. Suddenly rising and moving backward a little, she grasped me by the hair with a movement so sudden that I turned round in surprise and almost in fright, which brought me precisely into the spirit of the part, for she was brandishing a dagger. The passionate applause of the artists who were looking on resounded with exclamations of "Brava, Medea!" Then drawing me to her breast as though she were fighting to preserve me from the anger of Heaven, she evoked loud cries of "Viva, la Niobe!".

She took her inspiration from the antique statues, and without making any servile copy of them, recalled them to the poetical imagination of the Italians by improvised gesture. Others have tried to imitate Lady Hamilton's talent, but I doubt if anyone has succeeded. It is a business in which there is but a step from the sublime to the ridiculous. Moreover, to equal her success, the actor must first be of faultless beauty from head to foot, and such perfection is rare.'[62]

The above description makes it clear that however peculiar Lady Hamilton's performance would seem to a modern audience, she had mastered a difficult talent involving dexterity and a command of expression which, combined with her beauty, made her nearly impossible to imitate. Attempts were certainly made to copy her. John Thomas Smith describes the wife of the banker, Mrs Coutts, making a plainly unimpressive performance: 'One evening, when Nollekens accompanied Fuseli to dine with Mr and Mrs Coutts, the lively hostess, who had dressed herself as Morgiana, went round the room after dinner, presenting a dagger to the breast of every one of her visitors, as if she intended to stab them; and when she came to Nollekens, Fuseli was heard to cry out, "You may strike with safety;

Nolly was never known to bleed.''[63] Smith has only bothered to describe Mrs Coutts' attitudinising because of Fuseli's thin joke.

Lady Hamilton's attitudes, which required a high degree of skill and beauty, did not develop into a popular amateur art like the *tableaux vivants* which made their effect from elaborate costumes and properties rather than a flexible use of simple drapery. The tableaux, to judge by the photographs taken of the later performances, would certainly have benefitted from a little of Emma's facility of expression, but plainly a lack of expression was not considered a fatal handicap. The heirs of her imitations of classical statues were not so often amateurs as professionals. The *poses plastiques* of the music halls, which were mostly an excuse for showing young women in various states of undress, are an obvious and crude derivation of Emma's art, but the intention of these living statures was not always entirely erotic. Cooke's Circus, performing in Edinburgh in the 1840s, had the following attraction on their poster:

'a novel and interesting series of Tableaux, intended to convey the very imposing effect of:

MARBLE STATUES!!

or MODELS OF THE ANTIQUE, REPRESENTED BY MESSRS WILLIAM AND ALFRED COOKE

The piece has been prepared by a strict reference to Classic Authorities of eminence, both of our own times and those of antiquity; and from the peculiarity of colour and formation of Dresses employed, the representation has been universally allowed to be at once faithful, instructive, and pleasing. In this effort the Brothers are activated by the desire to exhibit a series of chaste Sculptural beauties, the fidelity of which, every lover and student of ancient and modern art will at once recognize and appreciate; and from the succcess which has attended former exhibitions, it is believed the piece will earn the approval of all who admire the execution of classic motion or posture. Mr COOKE, Jun will explain the arrangement of the subjects represented in this extraordinary performance.'[64]

The remarkable nineteenth-century fallacy that anything based on good taste and the best authorities would automatically be both desirable and educational, coupled with the belief that the lightly decorated truth of living figures in a tableau or attitude was as clever as a highly contrived and studied painting or sculpture, kept alive this curious art for far longer than the reality can ever have justified. The popularity of tableaux and the readiness to regard them as an art form paved the way for the pictorial photography which is now commonly regarded as a blight on the history of early photography.

The photographs illustrated here show photography imitating literary and historical painting. David Octavius Hill and Robert Adamson, who were in partnership from 1843 to 1847, produced a fairly small number of costume groups, some of which were almost certainly intended for use as book illustrations in an edition of Walter Scott's works. Their more elaborately posed groups used the services of Hill and his friends, who were experienced in theatrical performances and the setting up of tableaux (*ills 57–9*). With ex-

57 unknown subject, probably an illustration from
Walter Scott
with David Octavius Hill on the right
photograph by David Octavius Hill and Robert
Adamson
Scottish National Portrait Gallery

58 *Edie Ochiltree and Miss Wardour* from *The Antiquary*
with John Henning and Miss Cockburn
photograph by David Octavius Hill and Robert Adamson
Scottish National Portrait Gallery

posure times of up to three minutes, this experience was very necessary for any pose that could not be propped up with books under the elbow, head clamps, or convenient sticks or tables for the hands to rest on.

In the 1850s, the collodion process speeded up the exposure time so that pictorial photographers like Oscar Rejlander and William Lake Price could take pictures of amateur models in difficult poses and catch expressions far more readily. Rejlander did, however, use the services of 'Madame Wharton's *poses plastiques* group' for his ambitious allegorical photograph *The Two Ways of Life*, which involved not merely awkward poses but seminudity.[65] Lake Price's photographs are remarkable for his exact and precise rendering of detail and properties (*ill 60*) made possible by the new process.

David Wilkie Wynfield's photographs taken in the early 1860s show photography indulging in the fancy portrait. His photographs are close-ups emphasising the importance of the face, with the fancy historical costumes worn by his friends commonly reduced to a historical comment on his friends' features or perhaps their characters. Some of these portraits are successful and handsome (*ill 61*); others, peculiar. The photograph of Millais, which is one of the more extreme, shows him dressed as Dante (*ill 62*) and serves as a sidelight on the Victorian obsession with Florentine art and with Dante himself, and

59 *The Monks of Kennaquhair* from *The Abbot*
with William Borthwick Johnstone, William Leighton Leitch and David Scott
photograph by David Octavius Hill and Robert Adamson
Scottish National Portrait Gallery

60 *Don Quixote in his study*
photogravure by William Lake Price
Scottish National Portrait Gallery

62 Sir John Everett Millais (1829–1896) as *Dante*
photograph by David Wilkie Wynfield
National Portrait Gallery, London

also on the high opinion held of Millais' beauty. Millais was considered an extra-ordinarily handsome man from boyhood on-ward. Remarks like the following by William Blake Richmond surrounded him: 'He was like some knight of old who only needed to be clad in golden armour to appear the perfect Sir Galahad.'[66]

Interestingly enough, Millais was also Julia Margaret Cameron's idea of Sir Galahad but she did not succeed in persuading him to pose for her. Julia Margaret Cameron took up photography in 1863 with the overwhelming enthusiasm that she brought to everything she did. The only photographer she ever admired was David Wilkie Wynfield and there are some resemblances to his work in her close-up portraiture. Her best work was undoubtedly her portrait photography, with its close emphasis on the face of the sitter, and in this she achieved an impressive depth of characterisation. However, encouraged by G F Watts, she grew increasingly interested in pictorial photography and it is here that the flaws of her work are most visible. Mrs Cameron was a woman so heavily endowed with energy that she never discovered how to take short cuts. She liked her photographs on a large scale and used enormous and unmanageable glass plate negatives, and she also liked her photographs soft in focus. The resulting technique that she developed meant that her exposures took from three to seven minutes, far longer than the calotype process used twenty years earlier by Hill and Adamson, and ridiculous when compared to the few seconds' exposure used by Rejlander and Lake Price. In simple portrait or close-up photography, her sitters survived the experience and the photographs were often very good, but successful pictorial photography was a near impossibility. The girl who posed for Zenobia, Queen of Palmyra and for Vivien in the photograph of Vivien and Merlin (*ill 63*), which was part of a series intended to illustrate Tennyson's *Idylls of the King*, described being photographed: 'The studio, I remember, was very untidy and very uncomfortable. Mrs Cameron put a crown on my head and posed me as the heroic queen. This was

somewhat tedious, but not half so bad as the exposure. Mrs Cameron warned me before it commenced that it would take a long time, adding, with a sort of half groan, that it was the sole difficulty she had to contend with in working with large plates. The difficulties of development she did not seem to trouble about. The exposure began. A minute went over and I felt as if I must scream; another minute, and the sensation was as if my eyes were coming out of my head; a third, and the

63 *Merlin and Vivien*
with Charles Hay Cameron
photograph by Julia Margaret Cameron
National Portrait Gallery, London

64 *Boadicea*
photograph by Julia Margaret Cameron
National Portrait Gallery, London

back of my neck appeared to be afflicted with palsy; a fourth, and the crown, which was too large, began to slip down my forehead; a fifth—but here I utterly broke down, for Mr Cameron, who was very aged, and had unconquerable fits of hilarity which always came in the wrong places, began to laugh audibly, and this was too much for my self-possession, and I was obliged to join the dear old gentleman. When Mrs Cameron . . . bore off the gigantic dark slide, with the remark that she was afraid I had moved, I was obliged to tell her I was sure I had. This first picture was nothing but a series of "wobblings" and so was the second; the third was more successful, though the torture of standing for nearly ten minutes without a headrest was indescribable. I have a copy of that picture now. The face and the crown have not more than six outlines, and if it was Mrs Cameron's intention to represent Zenobia in the last stage of misery and desperation, I think she succeeded.'[67] The same sort of appalled exhaustion is obvious in the girl posing for Boadicea (ill 64). Mrs Cameron undoubtedly had a taste for the hollow-eyed facial collapse which was a natural result of her inept technique and probably equated it with the dark lack of expression that passed for ideal with artists like Burne-Jones.

Mrs Cameron's preference for a deliberately soft, blurred effect relates to the use of the dark gauze curtain in front of *tableaux vivants*. Both stem from a contemporary dislike of hard, bright, new paintings and a preference for dark varnished old masters. But the resemblance goes no further. Her work is distinguished from the fashion for tableaux by her lack of attention to background detail and costume and by her refusal to touch out mistakes. The distracting structure of her studio and her often crumpled draperies (*ills 63, 64*) make quite a few of her serious photographs merely depressing. The pictorial photographs of Hill and Adamson and Lake Price were allied more strongly with tableaux because Hill and Lake Price, as artists, were used to organising reality to make it into art. Julia Margaret Cameron, while taking a pride in the untouched truthfulness of her photographs, was nevertheless trying to get away from what the camera was actually looking at. By softening the focus she expected to lose awkward background detail, and if that failed she expected her admirers to ignore it; Hill and Adamson just moved the camera and the figures until the picture looked better. The difference in professionalism between the photographers may be seen in a comparison between *The Monks of Kennaquhair* and *Merlin and Vivien*. Hill's composition is a satisfactory grouping of light and shade, the background is solid and undistracting, and the materials used were good enough to fall in substantial folds. The seriousness of the artists posing for the group can be judged by William Leighton Leitch's having shaved off his hair for the occasion. Mrs Cameron's photograph employed inexperienced sitters in unironed clothing against a background of hard, illogical lines.

Julia Margaret Cameron's photography marks a veering away from the precise fake realism of pictorial photography but the art of tableaux continued throughout the century. The resemblance between the pictorial photography of the 1840s and 1850s and *tableaux vivants* was reinforced by the old-fashioned tendencies of their organisers. The royal tableaux of the 1880s and 1890s bear a similarity to mid-century painting, for example, the set piece of Bonnie Prince Charlie asleep in hiding (*ill 51*) is clearly related to Thomas Duncan's 1843 painting of the same subject. It seems possible that the practice of tableaux was a source of practical experience and inspiration to the pictorial photographers. It seems equally likely that the practice of photographing tableaux and turning them in this way into pictorial photographs increased the enthusiasm for tableaux, and their producers may even have organised them as much with an eye to the final photograph as to the temporary effect.

65 Queen Charlotte with her sons George, Prince of
Wales and Frederick, Duke of York (detail)
by Johann Zoffany
oil
*reproduced by gracious permission of Her Majesty The
Queen*

As a small boy George IV, then Prince of Wales, was painted by Zoffany with his mother and brother. Queen Charlotte is shown seated at her dressing-table elegantly clothed in the fashion of the day, but her sons are in more exotic garb: Frederick, Duke of York, still a toddler, is a be-turbaned figure in oriental dress, while George himself appears, as Telemachus, in 'Roman' costume, complete with spear and plumed helmet (*ill 65*). Even allowing for the convention of dressing figures in portraits in costume more timeless than contemporary clothes and for the delicate compliment to the Queen, in the oblique reference to the faithful Penelope it made possible, the choice for the two boys seems strangely flamboyant in the restrained atmosphere of their father's court. George III himself was, on occasion, painted in fancy dress—a few years later Zoffany portrayed him with his wife and six eldest children in Van Dyck costume—but, on the whole, he seems to have preferred the styles of his own time. It is noted in Farington's diary (28 December 1804) that when a portrait of George I was discovered in a lumber room he had it hung, commenting 'that it pleased him more than one painted by Sir Godfrey Kneller, because though the latter was better painted, it being in armour did not so truly represent the original as the picture now discovered which represented him in the dress he really wore'. The princes may have been painted in fancy dress to give their small figures some dignity but, whatever the reason, the choice was entirely suitable to the Prince of Wales. From a passionate interest in masquerade costume, worn as a young boy during the entertainments arranged by his governess,[68] he developed a love of dressing up which remained with him throughout his life.

Like his taste in building and collecting, into which he put much of the energy that was unable to find a political outlet during the long reign of his father, George IV's taste in dress was eclectic, frequently ostentatious, and often verging on the gaudy. Not having been trained, like his brothers, as a soldier or sailor, his interest in matters military was at first expressed solely by having himself painted in the appropriate clothes; the 1791

66 Danish fancy dress 'worn at the Prince Regent's fête'
plate from *La Belle Assemblée*, August 1819
Adam Dickson Esq

portrait by Mather Brown in the Royal Collection, for example, shows him in what is apparently an entirely imaginary uniform, possibly designed by himself. When in 1792-3, in the face of invasion, he was at last given a command as Colonel of the 10th Light Dragoons, he added interest to supervising their entirely home-based exercises by devising new uniforms for them.

In the meantime, he continued to enjoy attending and staging the fêtes for which his residences provided the perfect setting (*ill 66*). In 1789 he excited the admiration of Betsy Sheridan who, after seeing him and his brothers arrive at a ball dressed alike as highland chiefs, noted approvingly in her diary, 'nothing could be more elegant or becoming than their dress.'[69] The possibilities offered by so romantic and colourful a mode of dress clearly retained their appeal for, as recorded in Wilkie's portrait, George paid his new subjects the compliment of wearing full highland dress for a levée held at Holyroodhouse during his 1822 visit to Scotland. The outfit, complete with pistols, dirk and basket-hilted sword, was made specially for the occasion, the accessories mounted with gold and gems and magnificent down to the last detail, even to 'a pair of fine gold shoe Rosets with Vibrating centre made of Felegree gold studied all over with variegated Gems'.[70] The bill, not surprisingly, came to a massive £1,354.18.0.

Like others of his contemporaries, George IV had an eye to the costume of the past and was painted in various historical guises. By Cosway, he was depicted in Van Dyck dress and by Stroehling, in a work now lost, as the Black Prince; even a portrait of him in Garter robes is arranged to show to full advantage the doublet and trunk-hose beneath, which were based on those worn for ceremonial occasions in the late seventeenth century. It was not, however, until the age of fifty-eight that he found an event to give full rein to his showmanship: his coronation in July 1821, probably inspired by Napoleon's heavily theatrical crowning, was fantastically elaborate and costly, on a scale never since repeated in Britain. The coronation service was preceded by an assembly in Westminster Hall,

the great procession from there to the Abbey being led by the Royal Herbwoman and her attendants strewing flowers in its path, and was followed by a banquet for the male guests, the highlight of which was the King's champion riding fully clad in armour into the Hall to perform thrice the ceremony of throwing down the gauntlet.

Many of the participants wore costumes designed specifically for the occasion, with strong sixteenth- and seventeenth-century overtones. They were in accordance with the spirit of the times in that even everyday dress about 1820 incorporated Tudor and Stuart inspired features such as neck ruffs and puffed and 'slashed' sleeves. It is, in any case, usual for coronation ceremonial to emphasise aspects of the past as a reminder of the antiquity and continuity of the institution of kingship, but even so contemporary commentators were clearly puzzled by outfits which came remarkably close to fancy dress. Some features were tentatively attributed to the time of Elizabeth I, others to the court of Henri IV, and others still to the influence of Holbein; the *Observer of the Times* (21 July 1821) contented himself with the description, 'fantastic and antique costumes'.

The King himself was dressed in doublet and trunk-hose of cloth of silver, lavishly trimmed with gold, with a surcoat of velvet with hanging sleeves and an enormous plumed hat; overall was a velvet mantle of crimson and gold, with an immense train that caused him considerable fatigue despite the efforts of nine trainbearers. The King's immediate attendants and the peers were in white and gold, while those privy councillors who were not peers were in blue and gold. An outfit of the latter type, until recently in the possession of the Earls of Haddington and now in the National Museum of Antiquities of Scotland, was almost certainly worn by Thomas, Lord Binning, later 9th Earl of Haddington, who was created a peer in 1827, in the lifetime of his father, in recognition of his public services (*colour plate 2*). The full, short breeches and doublet with padded basque are in similar style to those of the King and are suggestive of the late sixteenth century, although of early nineteenth-century cut.

The material is blue satin, copiously trimmed with gold wire and sequins, and the matching cloak is trimmed with gold braid; white kid shoes with red heels and garters of gold lace finish the ensemble although, according to an engraving by Scriven, there would also originally have been a plumed hat. A virtually identical outfit, except that the materials and workmanship are of lesser quality, by tradition worn by the Rt Hon George Canning, is, like that of George IV, now in the Museum of London.[71]

'It will be remembered as the first and highly successful effort of a British monarch to make an amusement of the wealthy... a most picturesque and instructive illustration of the History of their Country, and a living gallery of the Portraits of the greatest and best of their ancestors'. Thus begins the volume compiled as a souvenir of the *bal costumé* given by Queen Victoria in 1842.[72] By the time of the accession of George IV's niece, the extravagance and ostentation of the Regency were out of place and, in a period of considerable public hardship, the 1838 coronation was celebrated with a subdued magnificence, the assembly and feast being entirely omitted. In keeping with the contemporary climate the court had a respectable, domestic atmosphere and even the three great fancy balls given by the young royal couple, which caused a considerable stir and added novelty to what would otherwise have been fairly monotonous court functions, were cloaked with purpose more serious than that of mere amusement.

Victoria and Albert led the first ball as Queen Philippa and Edward III (*colour plate 3*), with their immediate retinue in complementary fourteenth-century costumes. The evening must have required weeks, if not months, of preparation. According to J R Planché, Somerset Herald, antiquary, playwright, and author of the text of the commemorative volume, every effort was made to achieve historical accuracy, the materials being woven, accessories made, and jewellery remodelled especially for the event. Each of Coke Smyth's illustrations in Planché's book of the costumes is annotated with a list of the sources and authorities used: Victoria's velvet

and brocade dress and mantle were based on the effigies of Philippa of Hainault and Blanche de la Tour in Westminster Abbey and were enhanced with a crown of gold set with a 'jewel valued at £20,000 and a bejewelled stomacher incorporating gems said to be worth £60,000.' Equal care was taken with the appearance of the gentlemen: a number of them are depicted wearing the appropriate armour and weapons and if this is indeed an accurate indication of their dress on the night, dancing must have been a hazardous exercise.

According to Planché, it was the Queen's desire that every detail should be as correct as possible, but she complained about the preparations in a letter to her Uncle, Leopold King of the Belgians, 'so many silks and drawings... I who hate being troubled about dress am quite *confuse*'.[73] Although fond of pretty clothes, Victoria's inclination was towards comfort and convenience in dress, and it seems much more probable that the impetus came from her studious husband.[74] The Somerset Herald at least, was immensely proud of the resulting spectacle, claiming, 'The Antiquary and the Herald are courted for their information. The Book or Printseller finds a ready sale for his most costly publications. Artists are employed to copy, and Artizans of all sorts to reproduce the Armour or Costume of bye-gone days. Knowledge is acquired while money is circulated—Art advanced while Taste is improved.'[72] Against this, it is refreshing to discover that not all the participants in what was, after all, a social event regarded it so seriously: Planché himself records a lengthy dispute with the Earl of Cardigan who, intent upon appearing as a sixteenth-century figure, the Chevalier Bayard, resolutely preferred spangled tights and comfort to plate armour and accuracy.[75]

The approach to the successive fancy balls appears to have been a good deal less academic but care continued to be taken to publicise the benefit they conferred on the trade of the metropolis. The early years of the reign coincided with a period of industrial depression, including the silk industry which was faring badly in competition with France. At the time of Victoria's wedding there was considerable agitation in the press as to

67 The Hon Hugh Cholmondeley as *Sir Damian De Lacy* for the Waverley Quadrille at the 1842 royal ball
probably by Frederick Coke Smyth
watercolour, 43.2 × 33 cm
Michael Clayton Esq

whether her trousseau was entirely British made, as officially reported, or in reality had been acquired from France.[73] The balls were represented as a means of encouraging patronage of the native dress trade. In this respect, the 1845 *bal poudré* (*ill 68*) may not have fulfilled expectations, for the theme of the costume of exactly a century before offered the possibility of using ancestors' clothes and the Queen herself wore Queen Charlotte's lace; but the 1851 ball, at which costumes were limited to the Restoration period, must have provided ample compensation.

An impression of the Prince Consort's 1851 outfit can be acquired from Winterhalter's watercolour study (*ill 69*) and from contemporary descriptions of the materials. According to the *Illustrated London News*, he wore 'a coat of rich orange satin brocaded with gold, and with a green sprig; the sleeves turned up with crimson velvet, embroidered in gold and silver, with pink satin epaulettes upon the shoulder. A baldric of gold lace, embroidered with silver, and edged with a fringe of pink silk and silver bullion, carried the sword. The breeches were of crimson velvet with pink satin bows and gold lace'; lavender stockings and a sash of white and gold completed the picture.[76] It might be suspected that the effect reflected the florid taste of mid-nineteenth-century England more accurately than that of the court of Charles II. The report notes with pride that the costume was entirely British made, and that the silk brocade for the coat, 'the beauty

68 Prince Albert (1819–1861) in eighteenth-century dress, 1845
by J Brandard
lithograph, 30 × 20.9 cm
Adam Dickson Esq

69 Queen Victoria and Prince Albert in Restoration dress for their 1851 ball by Franz Xavier Winterhalter
watercolour, 55.9 × 44.4 cm
reproduced by gracious permission of Her Majesty The Queen

of which could not be surpassed in any country', was of Spitalfields manufacture, completed within twelve days of the order being placed.

On the same occasion, the Queen wore a particularly impressive collection of jewels: 'Her Majesty wore on the front of the body of the dress four large pear-shaped emeralds, of an immense value. Her Majesty's headdress was composed of a small diamond crown placed on the top of the head, and a large emerald set in diamonds with pearl loops on the side of the head.'[76] The dress itself, described as *le grand habit de cour* of the fashion of the Court of Louis XIV, introduced from France by Charles II', has been preserved, and even without the jewels is a sumptuous garment; perhaps significantly, no mention is made of its place of manufacture. The bodice and skirt (*colour plate 4*) are of grey moiré silk, trimmed with gold and silver lace and pink ribbon bows, falling open to reveal an underskirt of cloth of gold, further embellished with embroidery and silver fringes; the neck and sleeves were trimmed with antique lace but, even so, the composition and the narrow-waisted, full-skirted silhouette are unmistakably those of 1851.

On the death of the Prince Consort, the Queen plunged into retirement and costume of unrelieved black, and the frivolities of fancy dress were left to their children. In Edward, Prince of Wales, history had repeated itself, producing an heir-apparent with energy and intelligence, and the misfortune to have an exceptionally long-lived parent who was unwilling to allow him serious state employment. Once again, much of this energy found an outlet in social pursuits.

In July 1874, the Prince and Princess of Wales gave a fancy ball at their official residence Marlborough House. The evening, in which most of the royal family but not, of course, Victoria, participated, was organised by the Prince, with the aid of a committee which included Frederic Leighton, and with a thoroughness reminiscent of his father. Prominent guests were arranged in six quadrilles, the two headed by the host and hostess with historical themes and costumes based on

paintings. Alexandra led the Venetian quadrille in a ruby velvet gown of sixteenth-century inspiration with skirt-front and sleeves ornamented with puffed satin and embroidered with gold and jewels and the bodice hung with ropes of pearls; her husband led the Van Dyck quadrille which included the Duchess of Marlborough who 'had copied the famous Blenheim picture of Rubens' wife, and was all in black satin and lavender, a long veil flowing from her tufted Spanish head-

70 Arthur, Duke of Connaught (1850–1942) as the *Beast* for the Fairy Tale Quadrille at the Marlborough House Ball, 1874
by unknown photographer
reproduced by gracious permission of Her Majesty The Queen

1 Lady Charlotte Campbell (1775–1861) by Johann Wilhelm Tischbein oil, 197.2 × 134 cm.
Scottish National Portrait Gallery

2 Costume worn by Thomas, Lord Binning as a Privy Councillor at the coronation of George IV, 1821 blue silk trimmed with gold braid and sequins. *National Museum of Antiquities of Scotland*

3   Queen Victoria and Prince Albert as Queen Philippa and Edward III for their first
fancy dress ball, 1842 by Sir Edwin Landseer

oil, 131 × 111 cm. *Reproduced by gracious permission of Her Majesty The Queen*

4 Restoration style dress worn by Queen Victoria, 1851 grey watered silk trimmed with gold and silver lace, underskirt of cloth of gold. *Museum of London*

71 Edward, Prince of Wales (1841–1910) as the *Grand Prior of the Order of St John of Jerusalem* for the Devonshire House Ball, 1897 photograph from *The Devonshire House Fancy Dress Ball* *National Library of Scotland*

dress'.[77] Two other sets of dancers were in 'Pompadourish and pretty' crimson and white satin costumes as packs of cards. The scene was undoubtedly stolen by the ingenious appearance of one of the Prince's brothers, Arthur, Duke of Connaught (*ill 70*). The Duke and his partner headed the Fairy quadrille in the characters of Beauty and the Beast and he was clothed in a ruby velvet doublet and grey satin tights with 'a leopard's head and skin with gold claws, attached to his shoulders by large diamond stars';[77] later in the evening, in evidence of the transformation of the Beast, the leopard skin was discarded in favour of a small cap and long white feather. After the quadrilles had promenaded and danced they retired to supper in specially designed and decorated pavilions, one lined with tapestry and ranged with armoured figures and the other, which was smaller, completely lined with costly Indian carpets. The occasion caused the press to recall the elaborate balls staged by Victoria and Albert; but in one respect times had changed for there was no attempt to present the evening as anything other than a suitable pastime for the royal family of a prosperous nation at the centre of an empire: 'The pride of our people requires that there should be a well ordered magnificence in the lives of their Princes, and certainly His Royal Highness the Prince of Wales proved himself last night well descended from Kings whose courts have never been wanting in splendour.'[77]

Although the Prince and Princess of Wales gave only one major fancy dress ball, they were principal guests at a number of others. In 1871, Scott centenary year, they attended the Waverley Ball as Mary, Queen of Scots and the Lord of the Isles (*ill 2*). The beautiful Alexandra scarcely needed exotic garments to enliven her appearance, but Edward looked particularly well in historical costume, apparently enjoying playing the part and relishing

the opportunity to escape the dulness of late nineteenth-century men's dress. As one reporter commented on the evening at Marlborough House, 'the ladies were generally much less beholden to their antique costumes than the gentlemen, for latter day millinery is not so bad whereas latter day tailoring is poor work compared with Stuart and Georgian wardrobes.'[77] Edward's eye for dramatic possibilities is demonstrated by the outfit he had made for the Devonshire House Ball in 1897 and which is preserved in the collection of Messrs Berman and Nathan. In the character of 'Grand Prior of the Order of St John of Jerusalem' (*ill 71*), he wore doublet and hose of velvet embroidered with beads, a cloak of silk and cut velvet, with a feathered hat and long leather boots. The ensemble, although rich, is almost entirely black, an ideal choice for a stately but definitely middle-aged figure, and to which a background of the brightly coloured fabrics, lace, and resplendent jewels of the other dancers would have provided a perfect foil.

The Devonshire House Ball may have been the most elaborate of its kind: in celebration of Queen Victoria's Jubilee, seven hundred guests were entertained, all in fancy costumes and many organised in courts and processions which had been planned and rehearsed for weeks beforehand. Following a description of the Duchess of Devonshire's costume as Zenobia, Queen of Palmyra, embroidered with gold, silver and pearls and studded with precious stones, the reporter from the *Illustrated London News* added: 'It must be realised that such splendid masquerading is unsurpassable.'[78] Journalistic hyperbole it may have been, but it was also prophetic. The gaiety and brilliance of Edward's court and the leisure and prosperity on which they were based, passed with him and, like so much else, in the next century fancy dress balls were never quite the same.

72 Alexandra, Princess of Wales (1844–1925) as
Marguerite de Valois
for the Devonshire House Ball, 1897
photograph by Lafayette
reproduced by gracious permission of Her Majesty The Queen

73 The Duke and Duchess of York at the Devonshire House Ball, 1897
photograph by Lafayette
reproduced by gracious permission of Her Majesty The Queen
(next page)

73

The Wearing of Fancy Dress

74 *Soldat aux Gardes*
by de Frey after Paul Gavarni
lithograph, 32.5 × 23.4 cm
from *Nouveau Travestissemens*, no 37
Adam Dickson Esq

Most eighteenth-century gentlemen learnt about dressing up and masquerades from the obvious fount, which was Italy. The Roman carnival was an explicit occasion for licence, when the maskers were protected by the guards and given free rein to insult, caricature and bombard figures of dignity, such as priests, lawyers, and respectable married couples. Goethe described in his *Italian Journey* some of the details of the Roman carnival of 1787: '...an advocate elbows his way quickly through the crowd, declaiming as if he were addressing a court of justice. He shouts up at the windows, buttonholes the passers-by, whether in fancy dress or not, and threatens to prosecute every one of them. To one he reads out a long list of ridiculous crimes he is supposed to have committed, to another an exact tabulation of his debts. He accuses the women of having *cicisbei*, the girls of having lovers. He consults a book he carries with him, and produces documents—all this in a shrill voice and at great length. He tries to make everyone disconcerted and embarrassed... I did see one Pulcinella who was playing the role of a cuckold. His horns were movable, so that he could protrude and retract them like a snail. He would stop under the window of some newly married couple and show just the tip of one horn, then under another and shoot out both horns to their full length. Little bells were attached to their tips, which tinkled merrily whenever he did this. Now and then the crowd would notice him for a moment and roar with laughter.'[79]

A politer and more confined version of this was transplanted to England, especially to the London pleasure gardens such as Vauxhall. Not everyone, however, found it politer. In 1740, Horace Walpole preferred the Italian version in Florence: 'What makes masquerading more agreeable here than in England, is the great deference that is showed to the disguised. Here they do not catch at those little dirty opportunities of saying any ill-natured thing they know of you, do not abuse you because they may, or talk gross bawdy to a woman of quality.'[80]

Masked balls were both welcomed and condemned as opportunities for greater licence. A change of dress and a concealing mask often led to a relaxation of morals and an alteration in character. It can be no coincidence that the eighteenth century records a high number of proposals and elopements related to masquerades. At the first private masquerade in Scotland 'In order that proper decorum might be observed, several ladies of distinction were there unmasked.' Obviously, no high hopes were held of the occasion since it was also reported, 'the affair went off with more success than was expected.'[81] A public masquerade which was advertised by J Dunn in *The Edinburgh Evening Courant* in February 1786, which promised 'the strictest regularity and decorum',[81] was nevertheless doomed to failure by the attack made by William Creech, who published the following satirical advertisement in the same paper five days later:

'ADVERTISEMENT EXTRAORDINARY

M Slackjaw begs leave to inform the public, That she is to open a grand Masquerade warehouse, next door to the New Chapel, in Register Street, and a few doors from Dunn's Rooms. She every hour expects a very fine assortment of mask dresses, from Tavistock-Street and the Haymarket, London. Among others, a great variety of fancy dresses for ladies—such as, queens of various countries and sizes, sultanas, gypsies, vestal virgins, Columbines, Dutch milkmaids, hay-makers, fortune-tellers, ballad-singers, black and white nuns, nobodies, &c &c. Also a very becoming dress for a mad maid of Bedlam, with sparkling chains to sit easy and genteel—An elegant mourning habit for Jephtha's daughter—A Calista, with a fan, which may be easily seen through—A fine flesh coloured suit for Eve, as close as life—Also emblematical dresses for Fashion, Folly, Night and Aurora.

NB She had commissioned a Lucretia, but her correspondent says, no such character could be found at present in London.

For such ladies as choose more simple disguises, she has provided dominoes, jalousies—and also the smaller articles of dress, such as prominent bosoms and behinds, from the most enormous to the most moderate; and cool and airy masks of all kinds.

Convenient rooms will be ready, adjoining to the shop, for adjusting ceremonies, and settling plans, in case the apartments in the Hotel allotted for accommodation should be too crowded.—As the sole relish of this rational and elegant entertainment depends upon secrecy, customers may be assured that effectual means will be taken that no person in one chamber shall know what is going on in the next.

She has also been solicited by several of her friends to commission gentlemen's masks; but as fashionable gentlemen at present require little additional disguise in comparison with the ladies, she will not boast of the same variety in this department.—Those who have no characters to support (by much the greatest number, no doubt, upon such occasions,) may be supplied with various coloured dominos.—She has ordered a few excellent devils' masks, with gilded horns—a very good Don Quixote, with a shining Mambrino—a young Bacchus, but as the character is so common, particular decorations will be given—Several running-footmen, jockies, harlequins, chimney-sweeps—Many good dresses for Sir Johns and Jackie Brutes—men-midwives, with circumstantial printed advertisements—Calibans, Cupids, and Adonises in abundance—A very elegant dress for mad Tom, the blanket being worked like a modern shawl, and the crown filled with goose feathers in place of straw, the pole a Lochaber-axe—A very good knave of clubs, and a ninth of diamonds—A very fine dancing bear, and orang outang, fitted to represent human nature, either in its improved upright state, or in its primitive, upon all fours—NB with or without tails. With many other original characters too tedious to mention...'[83]

William Creech had high standards of morality and even higher standards of behaviour in women; he was an enthusiast for 'native innocence' and 'simple manners' and even at its purest a masquerade was liable to be short on both. The dark suspicion that masquerades were merely excuses for lewd behaviour is reflected fifty years later in another public advertisement for a masquerade proposed in Dublin in 1835: 'No impropriety, or breach of decorum, can possibly take place, when every individual composing the Maskers is exposed to the scrutiny of the Manager, the vigilance of the proper Police Officers, and the observation of the spectators in the Boxes and Gallery.'[84] In 1833, *The Times* reported a case tried before the Lord Mayor of a tailor's apprentice who attended a masquerade in a tavern in the 'kickseys' of a stolen Richard III outfit. Masquerades were adjudged yet another of the dangerous amusements suitable for the upper but not for the lower classes: 'The Lord Mayor said, that although he by no means wished to abridge the amusements of the people, he apprehended that masquerades among such classes as graced the amusements in question were extremely mischievous.'[85]

Masquerades and fancy dress parties gave rise to an internal morality. The wistful or possibly vain desire to attend a fancy dress party in a character opposite to your own was frequently attacked for its unsuitability. In 1711, the *Spectator* published a letter on the subject: '...I could wish, Sir, you could make them understand that it is a kind of acting to go in masquerade, and a man should be able to say or do the things proper for the dress in which he appears. We have now and then rakes in the habit of Roman senators, and grave politicians in the dress of rakes. The misfortune of the thing is, that people dress themselves in what they have a mind to be, and not what they are fit for. There is not a girl in the town, but let her have her will in going to a masque, and she shall dress as a shepherdess. But let me beg of them to read the 'Arcadia' or some other good romance, before they appear in any such character in my house. The last time we presented, everybody was so rashly habited, that when they came to speak to each other, a nymph with a crook had not a word to say but in the style of the pit, and a man in the habit of a philosopher was speechless, till an occasion offered of expressing himself in the refuse of the tyring-room. We had a judge that danced a minuet, with a Quaker for his partner, while half-a-dozen harlequins stood by as spectators. A Turk drank me off two bottles of wine, and a Jew eat me up half a ham of bacon. If I can bring my design to bear, and make the maskers preserve their characters in my assemblies, I hope you will allow there is a foundation laid for more elegant and improving gallantries than any the town at present affords, and consequently that you will give your approbation to the endeavours of, Sir, your most obedient servant.'[86]

Sir Walter Scott uttered a similar criticism of a ball in 1828: 'There were some good figures and some grossly absurd. A very gay cavalier with a broad bright battle axe was pointed out to me as an eminent distiller and another Knight, as he desired, armd in the black coarse armour of a cuirassier of the 17th century, stalked about as if he thought himself the very mirror of chivalry. He was the son of a celebrated upholsterer so might claim the broad axe from more titles than one.'[87] Incongruity in fancy dress was, of course, an easy target: George Du Maurier's joke of 1885 about the unlovely Mary, Queen of Scots conversing over the buffet with an inelegant Horace Walpole can only have been a commonplace (*ill 3*).

Occasionally, morality caught up with fancy dress parties in a most gratifying way, highly suitable for one of the more proper fairy stories. Elizabeth Gunning's marriage to the Duke of Hamilton in 1752 is one such event. 'My [Lady Charlotte Campbell's] mother once told me a little anecdote which I think proves better than volumes the different dispositions of the sisters. For a grand masked ball that was to take place at Chesterfield House, my mother had a magnificent Sultana's dress, sparkling with gold and jewels. She appeared in all that blaze of beauty before her sister, who had not yet attired herself in the habit of a Quakeress which she had chosen, and who no sooner cast her eyes on the brilliancy of the Sultana dress than she became perfectly dissatisfied with her own; my mother saw this and instantly proposed an exchange. As the modest Quakeress my mother became a duchess, for it was that night the Duke of Hamilton proposed to her.'[88] Whether he would have proposed to her as a Sultana is not, alas, in our power to test.

Understandably, not many people who attended fancy dress balls used them as an excuse for a display of unusual modesty—only

78

the most beautiful people could risk it. More
often they were seized as an opportunity to
break away from normal standards. It is
surprising how indecent in contemporary
terms women could become in the respectable
context of fancy dress, dressed with abnor-
mally short skirts showing an expanse not just
of ankle but of calf, or dressed as young men.
Nor was this confined to the demi-monde as
the more risqué plates of Paul Gavarni, who
was a leader in the revival of fancy dress in
France in the 1830s, might be supposed to be
(*ill 74*). Woodcuts in the *Illustrated London
News* of high society fancy dress balls show
high born and respectable ladies with their
calves exposed as well. The 'undress' aspect of
fancy dress was the butt of yet another Du
Maurier joke of 1878 about a young girl who
has gone to a ball as a salad (the dress is not
merely respectable but dull) conversing with
her uncle: ' "See there's Endive, and Lettuce,
and Spring Onions, and Radishes, and
Beetroot. Nothing wanting is there?"—Uncle
John "Hm—Ah!—perhaps a little more
Dressing, my Dear." '

Fancy dress had also the advantage of
providing opportunities to break away from
good taste. The rules of society might dictate
that an excessive display of jewellery, for
example, was in bad taste. Mrs Arthur Paget,
who attended the Devonshire House Ball in
1897 as Cleopatra, was plainly a woman
baulked in this manner. *Country Life*, reporting
on her costume, said, 'Her beauty is enhanced, too, by a perfect taste in dress', and
then went on to describe her costume: 'The
train of Mrs Arthur Paget's Cleopatra costume was of black crêpe de chine, embroidered with gold scarabaeus, and lined with
cloth of gold, and a sash of gauze tissue
wrought with stones and scarabaeus. The
bodice, glittering with gold and diamonds, was
held up on the shoulders with straps of large
emeralds and diamonds. The square headdress
was of Egyptian cloth of gold, the sphinx-like
side pieces being striped black and gold, and
encrusted with diamonds, and in the middle
of the forehead hung a large pearl from a
ruby. Above was the ibis with outstretched
wings of diamonds and sapphires, and beyond
were peacock feathers standing out, and the
back was all looped with pearls and amber.
The remainder of the headdress was of uncut
rubies and emeralds, all real stones, surmoun-
ted by the jewelled crown of Egypt. Round
the neck were row upon row of necklaces of
various gems, reaching to the waist, and a
jewelled girdle fell to the hem'[89] (*ill 75*).
Good taste had been shown the door for the
evening. It is also a pleasure to discover in
1833 A E Chalon, 'a large man with reddish
hair' who specialised in painting very delicate
and over-refined water colours of ladies, sending himself up by attending a ball as a
ballerina. 'The other night they went to a
fancy dress ball; Miss Chalon and her
brothers—she as a Swiss peasant, John as a
Spanish peasant, and Alfred as a ballet
dancer, though very dreadful and unfeminine he
looked in low neck, lace petticoats, white silk
stockings, satin shoes, and a Duchess de Berri
hat without a crown—just a brim turned up
with feathers and the hair dressed above.
They thought it great fun, but I thought it
shocking—this great man with his shaven red
beard and bare arms, but he was very
cleverly gotten up.'[90]

The desire to shine at a party, whether by

coming as Titania or Romeo or displaying extreme cleverness and wit by coming as a waste paper basket or the transatlantic telephone cable (*ill 76*), is natural enough. Fancy dress could be as creative an activity as any other art form. The landscape painter Sam Bough, visiting Vauxhall Gardens in an outfit designed by Nathan's to be an Inquisitor's costume, 'very tight fitting, and all ablaze with devices of innumerable little devils, enveloped with flames', turned himself into the Devil with the addition of a tail with an eel inside, which writhed and coiled in a fascinating manner until four in the morning, aided by Bough's sitting half in a fountain periodically to revive the animal.[91] A more whole-hearted performance which was staged more than once was contained in the old ladies created by Clementina Stirling Graham (*ill 77*). Miss Graham was an amiable and witty person, who cherished a taste for the old ladies of the sort described by Lord Cockburn: 'Their prominent qualities of sense, humour, affection and spirit were embodied in curious outsides; for they all dressed, and spoke, and did exactly as they chose...' It is easy to see that the temptation to perform as one of these old ladies, with their licence to dress and speak at will, must have been very great. She soon developed a reputation for her impersonations and was much in demand to entertain parties, some knowing her true identity and most ignorant but hypnotised by her long and rambling accounts of antiquarian pursuits (she claimed to own a flea that had come off Bonnie Prince Charlie, which she had had set into her watch and proposed to leave to the Society of Antiquaries) or a fantastic account of the rotation of crops on her land. One of her more satisfactory impersonations was inflicted on Francis, later Lord, Jeffrey who knew of her old ladies and asked her to come some evening when he had invited someone else to fool. Miss Graham came instead unannounced when she knew he was entertaining visitors. She came disguised as a toothless 'Lady Pitlyal' and treated him to a lengthy session covering, among other subjects, a convoluted point of law, an ancient prophecy she had just invented, where she could acquire a good set of false teeth, and

76 fashion plate
from *Courrier de la Mode, c* 1870
Adam Dickson Esq

the marriage of her daughter, the 'Rosebud of Pitlyal'. Only after her departure, when his dinner had probably spoilt, did Jeffrey realise who his visitor was. The pleasure of these impersonations is obvious enough, as is Miss Graham's reluctance to return to 'the humdrum realities of my own self' after the laughter and applause. Her performances were undoubtedly a very sophisticated piece of acting, as accomplished in their way as Lady Hamilton's attitudes.[92]

However, people most commonly dressed up without any acting ability in the hopes that they could take on the reflected charm of a period or person they admired, through the costume alone. The point that fashion only ever suits a limited number of people is of some importance at this period. The nineteenth century, which generally offered a woman a choice only between being beautiful or good, also brought out accurate works on historical costume, which enabled her to choose a dress from a large historical range to make her more beautiful. Lady Elizabeth Eastlake, who considered women's dress of the 1850s to be admirable, nevertheless realised that for those short on natural charm it was no help. 'Where is the advantage . . . of uncovering an ear which is less like a delicate shell than some ugly fungus? . . . or of showing an arm which may be like a stick, but certainly not of pink coral?' She remarked on the improvement that historical headdresses, especially, could make: 'Every fancy-ball brings out some striking or interesting face, generally in some such head-dresses as these, which the day before, seen in its own scanty suit, was overlooked as plain.'[93]

77 Clementina Stirling Graham (1782–1877)
by unknown artist
watercolour, 21.3 × 16.2 cm
Scottish National Portrait Gallery

IVANHOE   LE CHEVALIER NOIR
(Le Roi Richard cœur de Lion)

Costumes d'Ivanhoe

The Making of Fancy Dress

78 Lord Dunlo as *Ivanhoe* and Mr de Janti as the *Black Knight* for the Ivanhoe Ball, 1823
lithograph by Jobard after Felicité Lagarenne
from *Costumes d'Ivanhoe*, 1823
National Library of Scotland

80 fashion plate showing mediaeval fancy dress and fashionable dress
from *Petit Courrier des Dames*, 20 January 1836
Adam Dickson Esq

In the nineteenth century the subjects for ball costumes were as varied as they were numerous: themes might be topical, emblematical, humorous, or inspired by works of art or the contemporary theatre. But the dress of characters from the past, whether real or fictional, never lost its appeal. In some cases it is difficult for the modern observer to discern the difference between fancy dress and fashionable clothing. To some extent this was because the borderline between the two was blurred, the tendency towards historical revivals being particularly marked in women's dress of this period. Late in the 1890s, for example, Mlle Sans-Gêne commented on the subject of wedding dresses: 'I want Nellie to have a chiffon gown with a real lace train … while she hankers after the more solid attractions of white satin draped with lace and talks of copying some old Tudor picture, The women in London are mad today about copying old pictures. The Duchess of Devonshire is responsible for this I expect. I have no objection to this if the old picture be selected with a due regard for the appropriate, but Nellie is not a big woman, and I am sure she will look horrible with Tudor slashings and a wired lace collar, which is the immediate object of her dreams.'[94]

Especially early in the century, partly reflecting the state of knowledge of historical costume, the trend was towards the indiscriminate use of features from past centuries to create an 'antique' effect. The outfits, for instance, for the Ivanhoe Ball given in Brussels in 1823 by the Prince and Princess of Orange and attended by a number of British guests, were a romantic but entirely fanciful *mélange* as little related to the realities of the twelfth century as the atmosphere of Scott's novel (*ills 78, 79*). The men appeared in tunics of possible eleventh-century inspiration, with neck ruffs, puffed sleeves, bonnets and short cloaks drawn from the Tudors and Stuarts and pointed-toed footwear derived ultimately, perhaps, from fifteenth-century Burgundy, while a tall, draped headdress, presumably intended to represent the late mediaeval veiled henin but close in design to a contemporary peasant costume, was sufficient to transform a young lady in passably

VII

ALICIA
(Fille de Waldemer Fitzurse.)
Costumes d'Ivanhoe

WALDEMER FITZURSE
(Chevalier Normand.)

84

standard evening dress into a Norman maiden.

Even when greater accuracy was aimed for, historical fancy dress always retained the unmistakable stamp of the date of its making and wearing. This is equally true of representations of costumes actually being worn as of the ideals shown in fashion plates. The full sleeves, sloping shoulders and wide neckline of 1836 are faithfully mirrored in a design of that year for a mediaeval outfit (*ill 80*), Lady Elizabeth MacLeod and Mary Ferguson in the guise of Mary, Queen of Scots and Hermione at Lady Londonderry's ball in 1844 both exhibit clearly the ogee neckline and low pinched waist of the time (*ills 4, 81*). The reasons for this are twofold: however much the styles of the past are admired it is difficult, consciously or unconsciously, to escape the influence of current standards of beauty. Secondly, whichever period was represented, the methods of cut, construction and underpinning were those of the nineteenth century; it does not seem to have occurred even to the pedantic Planché to suggest to Queen Victoria and her ladies that they abandon their 1842 corsetry in favour of giving their mediaeval costumes the correct line. Logically enough, when the clothes of ancestors were pressed into service—and there are numerous examples of eighteenth-century dresses having been so used, presumably for the ever-popular *poudré* balls—they were generally altered to suit the favoured shape of the moment. Typical is a mid-eighteenth-century brocaded silk open robe worn at a St Andrew Boat Club fancy ball in Edinburgh shortly before 1900 (*ill 82*): the bodice was remodelled and boned and the dress was worn

81 Elizabeth MacLeod (d 1845) as *Hermione* at Lady Londonderry's ball, 1844
by Julius Jacob
watercolour, 55.9 × 40.6 cm
John MacLeod of MacLeod

without the support of the hooped petticoat that
would originally have shaped the skirt, bringing the silhouette closer to the sinuous outline
beloved of the turn of the century.

The demand for fancy dress was reflected in
the range of commercial enterprises involved
in what was, by the last quarter of the
nineteenth century, a veritable industry. The
making up of costumes was a recognised part
of the work of dressmakers of the time, however exalted, and some surviving pieces are
beautifully constructed examples of their craft.
Princess Alexandra's costume for her rôle as
Mary, Queen of Scots at the Waverley Ball of
1871 bears the label of Elise, London, and
may well have been remodelled by the same
hands for the Marlborough House Ball three
years later (*ills 2, 83*). Guests at the
Devonshire House Ball of 1897 were dressed
by the leading makers of the day, including
such distinguished names as Paquin and
Worth.

As an alternative, outfits both male and
female were made to measure by, or could be
hired from, theatrical costumiers. The results,
if a shade closer to stage costumes, are
scarcely less well made than those of the dressmakers (*for example, ill 85*). A number of
theatrical costumiers were patronised by the
royal family, including M and Mme Alias,
who dressed the Prince of Wales for the
Devonshire House Ball (*ill 71*), and Nathan's
who received a royal appointment in 1888 in
recognition of their services, amongst others,
in costuming *tableaux vivants* at Osborne.[95] An
advertisement of 1839 for L and H Nathan
describes their business as 'Masquerade
Warehouse and Fancy Costumes', and although they later enlarged their activities to

83 fancy dress worn by Princess Alexandra, originally
as *Mary, Queen of Scots* in 1871 and remodelled
possibly in 1874 for the Marlborough House Ball
by Elise of Regent Street, London
claret-coloured velvet with sleeves and front of
blue-green satin trimmed with gold lace and paste
jewels.
Museum of London

84 Winifred, Duchess of Portland as the *Duchess of Savoy* for the Devonshire House Ball, 1897
photograph from *The Devonshire House Fancy Dress Ball*
National Library of Scotland

85 seventeenth-century style costume worn by the Earl of Gifford *c* 1900
by L and H Nathan
cream silk trimmed with gold braid
National Museum of Antiquities of Scotland

86 fashion plate with fashionable dress and an outfit for *Diana*
by Jules David
from *Le Moniteur de la Mode, c* 1865
Adam Dickson Esq

87 seventeenth-century and Turkish costumes with fashionable dress
by Louis Berli after Heloise Leloir
from *L'Iris*, 1857
Adam Dickson Esq

include work for the professional stage, military and naval outfitting, and court wear (*ill 88*), the provision of garments and accessories for amateur theatricals and fancy balls represented a substantial proportion of their trade (*ills 89, 90*).

Both costumiers and dressmakers also made outfits for children and these small costumes seem to have been little less elaborate than those of the adults. One occasion in which Nathan's had a large hand was the fancy dress ball held at the Mansion House in London in 1887 in honour of Queen Victoria's Jubilee. It began with a procession of one hundred and fifty children representing the sovereigns since the Conquest and their most notable subjects. The star part—that of Queen Elizabeth I—was played by the Lord Mayor's daughter, who was celebrating her ninth birthday: 'The costume worn by her small Majesty at the Mansion House was very complete and historically correct. It consisted of a bodice and train of that rich material known as silver brocade—a pattern fully worked in silver thread on a white satin ground—with full sleeves of the same, slashed for plain white satin to be drawn through; a white satin stomacher and petticoat, much adorned with pearls and diamonds; a big and elaborate ruff and a wonderfully curled and twisted head of auburn hair with a royal diadem set on top, and a "bob" pearl drooping on to the forehead.'[96] A further illustration of the care lavished upon children's fancy dresses is provided by a sixteenth-century style suit for a boy, worn by one of the family of the Earl of Crawford and Balcarres, perhaps about 1880. The outfit, although without a maker's label, appears to be the work of a professional

88 advertisement for L and H Nathan
from Ardern Holt, *Gentleman's Fancy Dress*, 1882

90 advertisement for Mrs Samuel May
from Marie Schild, *Old English Costumes*, 1884

89 advertisement for Auguste & Cie
from Marie Schild, *Album of Fancy Costumes*, 1885

costumier and is closely based upon an Italian picture *c*1550 in the National Gallery, London, *Portrait of a Boy in Red*[97] (*ills 91, 92*). The doublet and breeches are carried out in fine red silk trimmed with narrow gold braid. The garments are lined and the doublet is boned to give a firm finish at the waist and although the cod piece has been omitted and the material ruched rather than slashed, the general effect is very similar to the original. Over this was worn a gown of midnight blue velvet, the embroidery faithfully copied from the picture in gold braid.

For those who wished to make their own costumes, or dressmakers who lacked inspiration, there were ideas published in the form of fashion plates and, by the 1880s, complete books of suggestions and advice. Ardern Holt's *Fancy Dresses Described: or what to wear at fancy balls* (*ill 95*), which details several hundred costumes for women and children, was in its third edition by 1882 and had passed through a further three by 1895. The book was published by Debenham and Freebody, who would make to order any of the outfits described, but it also seems to have been used by other dressmakers.[98] The author did not aim for complete accuracy 'for, as a rule, the historical dresses worn on such occasions are lamentably incorrect ... [and] with regard to national costumes, no one would probably view them with more curiosity than the peasantry they are intended to portray' but offered instead advice, for example, on hairdressing

91 *Portrait of a boy in red*
     by unknown artist
     oil on panel, 128 × 61 cm
     National Gallery, London

and how to avoid the worst errors. He also made suggestions as to the characters most suitable to the age, figure, and disposition of the intending maskers, a theme he returned to in a separate book on men's costume, *Gentlemen's Fancy Dress: How to Choose it* (1882). Another series of books was published by Samuel Miller of Covent Garden under the authorship of Mme Marie Schild. Her *Album of Fancy Costumes*, produced about 1883, aimed to sell designs to readers. Customers could obtain a coloured print of any of the costumes described or, for 6s 6d, a paper model consisting of 'an exact representation of the costume made in coloured paper and accompanied by a flat pattern cut in plain paper. The pattern can be cut out to fit the intending wearer, and a very fair fit assured.'

There was also commercial activity in providing the accessories which completed the outfits. Debenham and Freebody advertised that they would provide to order 'Boots, Shoes, Sandals, Gilt Ornaments, Gems, Daggers, Helmets, Masks, Powder, Swords, Wigs and any other article required', while the books of costumes contain advertisements for all manner of services and products from 'Cirrosine Magic Curling Fluid' to real seaweed 'suitable for draping and trimming the costumes of Sea Nymphs, Undine, Water Spirits etc'. Many costumes were little more than contemporary evening dress thinly disguised and relied heavily upon accessories to convey the character: a pair of wings fastened

92 sixteenth-century style costume based on no 91
red silk and dark blue velvet trimmed with gold braid
Earl of Crawford and Balcarres

94 David, Master of Lindsay (1871–1940)
miniature by Reginald Easton, 1876
watercolour on ivory, 12.1 cm high
Earl of Crawford and Balcarres

93 fancy dress worn by David, Master of Lindsay and
probably by the Hon James Lindsay
red silk trimmed with gold braid, with silk brocade
tabard
Earl of Crawford and Balcarres

to the shoulders and a trimming of down, sealed envelopes and stuffed birds might transform a white dress into Pigeon Post (*ill 96*), while Diana might wear a sash of fur and carry a hunting horn and quiver and bow, with a crescent ornament in her hair. Madame Schild recommended taking this a stage further by the acquisition of the appropriate jewellery—with an owl motif for Night, 'gold quiver ear-rings' for Diana, a Water Lizard Brooch for a Water Nymph, and so on—from Messrs Thornhill's range.

To the twentieth-century eye, the most remarkable aspect of fancy dress from the last century is the care and expense lavished upon it. An extreme example is recorded in Jean Philippe Worth's anecdote about his famous father who had agreed, as a special favour, to create the Duke of Marlborough's costume for the Devonshire House Ball (*ill 97*). The result was 'a Louis XV costume of straw-coloured velvet embroidered in silver, pearls and diamonds. The waistcoat was made of a magnificent white and gold damask that was an exact copy of a very rare old pattern. Each pearl and diamond was sewed on by hand, and it took several girls almost a month to complete this embroidery of jewels. Had the Duke not insisted that his costume be perfection, we should never have dared put such costly work on it. In spite of his orders about elegance, when I came to make out his bill, I was almost afraid to begin it. But at last when I got it totaled, it came to five thousand francs ... or one thousand dollars for a masquerade to be worn for one evening. However, when damask is especially manufactured and jeweled embroidery hand-stitched, there is no escaping a bill that is quite as splendid in its way as the costume for which it is rendered.'[99] The Duke of Marlborough's outfit was clearly exceptional, even for the late nineteenth century. Nonetheless, surviving costumes are remarkably well-made for garments intended to be worn once, or at most two or three times, and retain a charm and brilliance even without the mass of jewels with which they were so often worn. One explanation is perhaps that fancy dress offered the leisured section of society not only the agreeable pastimes of planning costumes and practising quadrilles

95 *The Hornet*
from Ardern Holt, *Fancy Dresses Described*, 1882

but also added an element of novelty to social occasions and an opportunity for the display of both wealth and the person beyond even that offered by contemporary evening dress. Most of its wearers would no doubt have agreed with Ardern Holt, 'there are few occasions when a woman has a better opportunity of showing her charms to advantage than at a Fancy Ball'.[100]

105 Sir Francis Sykes
and family
by Daniel Maclise
watercolour,
113 × 64.8 cm
F J B Sykes Esq

The Eglinton Tournament

106 William Black (1841–1898)
by John Pettie, 1877
oil, 128.3 × 80 cm
Glasgow Art Gallery

*N*o part of George IV's elaborate and theatrical coronation in 1821 seems to have made a greater impression upon the participants than the ceremony that took place during the banquet which followed the crowning. At the end of the first course the King's Champion, in full armour, rode into Westminster Hall and three times threw down his gauntlet as a challenge to anyone who disputed the sovereign's right to the throne. The effect, in such a setting, was remarkable: 'Every fair bosom felt an indescribable sensation of mingled surprise, pleasure and apprehension. It seemed as if they were impressed with a conviction that the defiance might not prove an empty ceremony; that a trial as severe as that of Ivanhoe in the presence of his future Sovereign at Ashby might await the challenger ... For a moment the fast-fading spirit of chivalry re-asserted itself within these walls over minds which the place and occasion had rendered vividly susceptible of impressions connected with the records of our earlier history.'[101] Spectacular as it was, the cost of the whole occasion had been astronomical and when, seventeen years later, George's niece Victoria was to be crowned it was decided that such expenditure was unjustifiable. Despite protests about back-door methods of enthroning the Queen and the loss to trade, the 'Penny Coronation' took place with much-reduced ceremony, the banquet, and hence the appearance of the Champion, being entirely omitted.

It happened that the Knight Marshal of the Royal Household, Sir Charles Lambe, who should have marshalled the Champion, had a son who had been passionately interested in all things mediaeval since he was a small boy, and a step-son, the 13th Earl of Eglinton, who was both a keen sportsman and one of the wealthiest young men in Britain. The suggestion was made that in compensation for having been unable to fulfil his capacity at the coronation, there should be mediaeval games staged at the next private race meeting at Eglinton Park, the Ayrshire home of the Earl, during which someone should appear in armour and perform the ceremony of the challenge. From these small beginnings grew the idea of recreating a full-scale tournament at which the Earl and his friends, suitably mounted and attired, would compete for the victor's crown in the presence of their ladies, headed by a Queen of Beauty, and all in appropriate costume.

The scale of the preparations for the Eglinton Tournament of August 1839 was exceptional, but the idea was by no means unique. Tournaments had been held in Europe at various times since the seventeenth century:[102] one had been given, for example, in Vienna in 1814 in honour of the Allied Sovereigns, at which twenty-four knights, watched by their diamond-bedecked ladies, had tilted at wooden heads and performed manoeuvres,[103] and in 1827 there had been mediaeval games at Firle Park, the home of Captain Gage, who participated in the 1839 event. Nor was Charles Lambe the younger alone in his interest in mediaeval life. With the immensely successful *Ivanhoe* (1819), Sir Walter Scott had judged the taste of his public to perfection: the Gothic revival had reached full spate and produced a generation bred on tales of chivalry and the knights of King Arthur, and which inhabited neo-historical mansions plenished with furniture in the appropriate style and hung with portraits of themselves in period costume. A delightful example of the latter is the watercolour by Daniel Maclise, first exhibited in 1837, of Sir Francis Sykes and his family. *Pater familias* is shown clad in plate armour progressing, lance over shoulder, down a stone staircase preceded by his three sons dressed as pages, his small daughter, in something approaching seventeenth-century costume, and his wife, the contemporary outline of whose dress is given a mediaeval flavour by the addition of a fur-edged mantle, an ornate rosary and a rich stole in place of the fashionable shawl[104] (*ill 105*).

Armour was collected by the owners of Gothic residences, by antiquarians such as Sir Samuel Rush Meyrick who was responsible for the new display of the suits in the Tower of London in 1828, and by artists such as Sir Joseph Noël Paton and John Pettie who acquired it both for its own sake and for use in historical pictures and portraits of friends

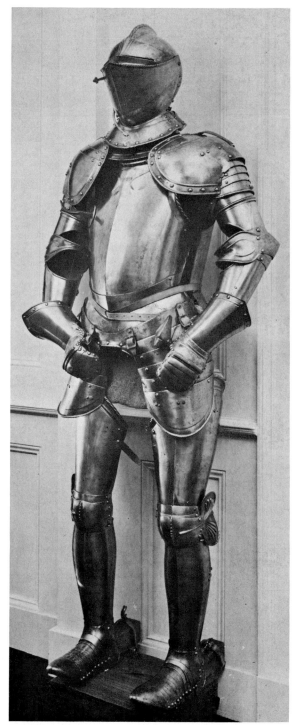

107 armour worn by Captain J O Fairlie as the *Knight of the Golden Lion* at the Eglinton Tournament composite suite of French and German armour made by Samuel Pratt (the nineteenth-century paint has recently been removed)
Captain D O Fairlie

(*ill 106*). In particular, it appealed to nineteenth-century imaginations as an example of the (supposed) excellence of the hand-made articles of the past as compared with the increasingly machine-made goods of their own day. To quote George Frederic Watts: 'The untiring interest, the pains, the love bestowed upon the perfecting and decorating of almost all objects of daily use, even when the service required was most material, is one of the most striking points of difference between ancient or mediaeval and modern life. Armour is an example. In unaffected, unconscious artistic excellence of invention, approaching more nearly to the strange beauty of nature, especially as presented to us in vegetation, mediaeval armour perhaps surpasses any other effort of human ingenuity.'[105] To meet the demand for armour, there were dealers, notably, early in the century, Samuel Luke Pratt of Bond Street. In 1838 he set up an extensive display at 3

108 J O Fairlie of Coodham, Ayrshire, in the armour
he wore at the Eglinton Tournament
by unknown photographer, *c* 1850
Captain D O Fairlie

109 *The Presentation of the Knight*
lithograph by K Loeillot after James Henry Nixon
from John Richardson, *The Eglinton Tournament*,
1843
Scottish National Portrait Gallery

Lower Grosvenor Street, London. Suits and weapons were shown in a 'truly Gothic apartment' furbished to the designs of L N Cottingham with, seated at a table, 'six grim figures, in full armour, apparently in debate' forming a memorable centrepiece.[106]

In view of the success of Pratt's exhibit, it is not surprising that the Earl of Eglinton and his friends should have turned to him in their search for authenticity, both for equipment and advice. The work of assembling the armour alone for Lord Eglinton, thirteen companions and various guests, including the Marquis of Londonderry (*King of the Tournament*) and Louis Napoleon (*Knight Visitor*), occupied many months. At the time, it was believed that almost all of it was original: 'some of it is as venerable as the days of Richard II, and none is more modern than the days of Queen Elizabeth. All in fact that the moderns have done is patching or repainting the rents which time may have left open; but on the whole the various plates and pieces comprising the suits were firm and substantial and showed little marks of decay.'[107] A number of the pieces can still be identified and although the authenticity of some of them is now in doubt it is difficult to know how far Pratt was aware of this. A fifteenth-century style suit, for example, worn by the Marquess of Waterford (*Knight of the Dragon*) and now in Windsor Castle, was bought by the Tower of London in 1840 but is considered to be a fake.[108] The armour worn by a local landowner, Captain J O Fairlie of Coodham, Ayrshire, who appeared as the *Knight of the Golden Lion*, is still in the possession of his family (*ill 107*). The suit, today recognised as a composite but which has been worked to

give it a uniform appearance, was painted for the occasion in black with raised gilded motifs and a lion on both breast plate and shield. It has since been cleaned but something of its appearance in 1839 is recorded in a photograph of Captain Fairlie wearing it about fifteen years after the event (*ill 108*).

Apart from the combatants themselves, there were esquires, banner-bearers, and other attendants to be dressed in suitable style, and again Pratt seems to have undertaken much of the work. Most impressive of all was the entourage of Viscount Glenlyon, later 6th Duke of Atholl, who took on the character of the *Knight of the Gael*. Apart from his armour, complete with crest, and the caparisons of his mount (*ill 109, foreground*) which can be seen at Blair Castle, there was equipment for a retinue of seventy-eight officers and men, all in tartan. An outfit, probably worn on the occasion by John Balfour of Balbirnie, one of Lord Glenlyon's two esquires, has been preserved. It consists of a tunic of Murray of Atholl silk tartan (red on a dark green and blue ground), padded to support a breast plate, and with undersleeves and bonnet of red silk tartan, and buff boots.[109] Pratt was also responsible for construction on site at Eglinton. The requests for tickets to view the event had by far exceeded expectations and stands, including the pavilion of Lady Seymour (the *Queen of Beauty*) (*ill 113*), were erected around the lists to accommodate over two thousand spectators. Visitors were asked to appear in fourteenth- and fifteenth-century dress,[110] although on the day costumes of all varieties were seen: 'there was the scarlet and the waving plumage of military officers, the slashed and fanciful doublet of the Spaniard

110 *General View of the Lists*
lithograph by K Loeillot after James Henry Nixon
from John Richardson, *The Eglinton Tournament*,
1843
Scottish National Portrait Gallery

III *The Queen of Beauty advancing to the Lists*
lithograph by Edward Corbould
from Edward Corbould, *The Tournament at Eglinton
Castle*, 1840
National Library of Scotland

and the Italian, and all the gay and striking colours with which our forefathers—in that respect so unlike their descendants—loved to adorn their persons',[111] while amongst the ladies 'might be seen some stately dame in the attire of the Elizabethan age exchanging words with the less magnificent but not less elegant form of a Flora McDonald'.[112] It was planned that the tournament be followed by a banquet and ball and for this a pavilion, reputedly 375 feet long, was specially built.

The gentlemen exchanged their armour for evening costume of more or less late mediaeval aspect. For Lord Glenlyon, Pratt had made up a rich costume of tartan velvet with cap and plume, and pantaloons of scarlet silk,[113] while the *Knight of the Golden Lion*, if a portrait painted in Rome in 1870 is accurate, was transformed into a troubador: the picture shows Captain Fairlie's son dressed in such a costume and, by tradition, this is the evening outfit worn by his father at Eglinton in 1839

112 *The Mêlée*
lithograph by Edward Corbould
from Edward Corbould, *The Tournament at Eglinton Castle*, 1840
National Library of Scotland

113 Lady Elizabeth Seymour as the *Queen of Beauty*
by J Bouvier
lithograph, 40.7 × 24.8 cm
National Portrait Gallery, London

(*ill 114*). Nothing of this outfit survives except the blue silk scarf, ornamented with a lion, shown at the left of the portrait.

'The world has been startled from its lethargy. After centuries of repose, each distinguished beyond its predecessor for an increasing tendency to utilitarian dullness, the age of chivalry, with its splendid pageants has again come round; and the eyes of the lover of the romantic have been favoured with the sight of a real tournament.'[114] Thus begins an account of the tournament, published in Edinburgh soon after the occasion. But neither this nor the lithographs produced by the various artists who attended to record the scene[115] give an impression of the disaster which overtook the event. The tournament was scheduled to begin on Wednesday, 29 August and visitors by the thousand arrived at Eglinton by rail, road and sea. Accommodation was stretched far beyond its limits, roads became blocked with the traffic, and the procession of participants from the Castle to the lists proved difficult to marshal and was hours late. None of this would have mattered but for the intervention of the weather. The month before, a rehearsal of the jousting had been held in London in perfect conditions and provided a spectacle which, according to one observer, might have been 'sufficient to cause the canonised bones of the author of Ivanhoe "to burst their cerements" and stalk to St John's wood' to witness the scene.[116] On the day, however, what began as a drizzle became persistent torrential rain, flooding the lists, and the stands and banqueting hall which had been roofed with nothing more substantial than oil cloth, and reducing the scene to the ridiculous: 'Clad in complete steel, with casque and nodding plume on his head, mounted on an unexceptional steed, that bore his burden bravely, the Marquis [of Londonderry], as far as looks went might have posed to an artist as a veritable re-incarnation of a *preux* chevalier, or a knight of olden time. But *horresco referens*! The rain beat so heavily upon him that his knightly nature could not endure it, and, to shield himself and his finery from the pitiless downpour, he hoisted a large umbrella over his head, and brought the fifteenth and nineteenth centuries into inharmonious and ludicrous juxta posi-tion, and forced the Queen of Beauty herself, and all who beheld the show, into irreverent but natural laughter.[117] Against such odds, to proceed was hopeless and the day's events were abandoned, leaving the drenched and bedraggled audience to return home as best it might.

The tournament did eventually take place. By the end of the week the weather had changed for the good and, after two days' frantic efforts to repair the lists and pavilions, both the jousting and the banquet went for-ward. The Earl of Eglinton was declared the victor, the banners and shields of the com-batants were presented to him to be hung in the Castle, and a subscription was raised to present him with a silver trophy in memory of an event he would perhaps rather have for-gotten. The trophy (*ill 115*), weighing 1600 ounces and nearly four feet high, was de-signed by Cotterill and made by Garrard of London, and shows the victor, in suitably Gothic surroundings, being presented to the Queen of Beauty by the Knight Marshal.[118]

In one sense the Eglinton Tournament had been a disaster—an extravaganza, expensive

114 J O R Fairlie of Myres in the evening dress worn by his father at the Eglinton Tournament
by F Guidi, Rome, 1870
oil, *c* 100 × 60 cm
Captain D O Fairlie

even beyond the intentions of the wealthy Earl, reduced to farce by the rain. After four days of cramped conditions and bad weather, reporters were understandably 'utterly weary of the Tournament and of frivolous and scarcely picturesque unrealities'.[119] Even so, for some the eventual spectacle had been worth seeing, while others considered its significance as more than that of a fancy dress occasion, rather an attempt to recreate and experience the true spirit of a better age. The next year, Peter Buchan published a defence of the event in the form of a dialogue between Sir David Lindsay of the Mount and King James in Elysium, commenting:

'The attempt to revive, at the present day, the chivalrous pastime of "the Tournament" has been derided by the cold "philosophy" of a money-getting utilitarian age. Yet, let me ask, are the mass of the people happier because the "age of chivalry has past", and, in what was once "Merry England", the sordid, heartless, sensual doctrines of utilitarianism have triumphed over sentiment, and nearly extinguished the fine impulses and generous instincts of man's nature?'[120]

115 The Eglinton Tournament trophy, given by the participants in the Tournament to the Earl in 1843 by Cotterill
silver, *c* 1 metre high
illustration from *The Illustrated London News*, 1843

THE EGLINTOUN TESTIMONIAL.

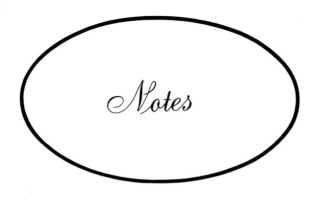

Notes

1 George Romney in 1787 quoted in William Hayley, *The Life of George Romney*, 1809, p 123.

2 William Hazlitt quoted in William Whitley, *Art in England 1821–1837*, 1930, p 205.

3 *Spectator*, 28 July 1711.

4 Allan Cunningham, *Lives of the Most Eminent British Painters, Sculptors and Architects*, 1833, vol VI, p 163.

5 George Frederic Watts, 'The Present Conditions of Art' in M S Watts (editor), *George Frederic Watts*, 1912, vol III, p 153.

6 Lady Elizabeth Eastlake, 'The Art of Dress' in *Music and The Art of Dress*, 1852.

7 Mary Woodall (editor), *Letters of Thomas Gainsborough*, 1961, pp 51–3.

8 Ardern Holt, *Fancy Dresses Described*, 1882, p 53.

9 Ibid, 6th Edition, *c* 1895–6, p 122.

10 John Thomas Smith, *Nollekens and his times*, 1828, vol II, p 393.

11 Quoted in Lionel Cust, *Notes on the Authentic Portraits of Mary Queen of Scots*, 1903, pp 137–8.

12 Mrs Paget Toynbee (editor), *The Letters of Horace Walpole*, vol I, 1903, p 181.

13 Accounts of this appear in Vicomte de Reiset, *Marie-Caroline Duchesse de Berry 1816–1830*, 1906, pp 197–8, and *Petit Courrier des Dames*, 10 March 1829.

14 'Irish Sketches by Two Subs, 4. Our Fancy Ball', *Illustrations, a pictorial review of knowledge*, May 1888.

15 Walter Scott, *The Abbot*.

16 Horace Walpole, op cit, vol VII, 1904, p 392.

17 Ibid, vol VI, 1904, p 81.

18 Mrs Delany, 'Autobiography' quoted in Harry Graham, *A Group of Scottish Women*, no date, p 147.

19 Horace Walpole, op cit, vol XV, 1905, p 1.

20 Captain Hall, 'Journal', quoted in John Gibson Lockhart, *Life of Sir Walter Scott*, 1893, p 529.

21 Allan Cunningham, *The Life of Sir David Wilkie*, 1843, vol II, p 353.

22 John Gibson Lockhart, op cit, p 755.

23 For a discussion of the popularity of Hussar dress, see Aileen Ribiero, 'Hussars in Masquerade', *Apollo*, February 1977.

24 Article on Edward Wortley Montagu by J M Rigg, *The Dictionary of National Biography*, 1894.

25 George Frederic Watts, op cit, p 162.

26 *Catalogue of Mr Geddes's Pictures Now exhibiting in Bruce's Great Room*, 1821, p 9.

27 W D Mackay and Frank Rinder, *The Royal Scottish Academy*, 1917, p 14.

28 John Zephaniah Bell, 'The Taste of the Day', *Fraser's Magazine for Town and Country*, vol LVI, 1857.

29 Lady Elizabeth Eastlake, *Memoir of Sir Charles Lock Eastlake*, 1870, p 146.

30 Adela Geddes, *Memoir of the Late Andrew Geddes, Esq, ARA*, 1844, p 10.

31 Thomas Landseer (editor), *Life and Letters of William Bewick*, 1871, vol II, p 231.

32 George Vertue, 'Notebooks', *Walpole Society*, vol xxii(III), 1934, p 125.

33 Quoted in Gladys Scott Thomson, *Letters of a Grandmother*, 1943, pp 118, 120.

34 Sir Joshua Reynolds, 'The Seventh Discourse' in Roger Fry (editor), *Discourses Delivered to the Students of the Royal Academy*, 1905, p 216.

35 Ibid, 'The Sixth Discourse', p 167.

36 Allan Cunningham, op cit, vol III, p 177.

37 Lady Elizabeth Eastlake, 'The Art of Dress' in *Music and The Art of Dress*, 1852.

38 James Robinson Planché, *The History of British Costume*, 1834, p 323.

39 John Sobieski Stuart and Charles Edward Stuart, *The Costume of the Clans*, 1892, p. 108.

40 Quoted in John Telfer Dunbar, *History of Highland Dress*, 1962, p 123.

41 Joseph Farington, *The Farington Diary*, vol III, 1924, p 291.

42 A M W Stirling, *The Richmond Papers*, 1926, p 49.

43 Sold at Christie's, 2 April 1965, lot 89.

44 Sir Joshua Reynolds, op cit, 'The Seventh Discourse', pp 215–6.

45 E G Forbes, letter to Robert Chalmers, 13 August 1772, manuscript, National Library of Scotland, Acc 3081.

46 Sir Joshua Reynolds, op cit, 'The Seventh Discourse', p 198.

47 Johann Wilhelm Tischbein, *Aus Meinem Leben*, 1956, pp 296–7.

48 Sir Joshua Reynolds, op cit, 'The Third Discourse', p 60.

49 Quoted in Leonée and Richard Ormond, *Lord Leighton*, 1975, p 85.

50 Quoted in Allan Cunningham, op cit, vol II, p 216.

51 Lady Charlotte Campbell, *Diary Illustrative of the Times of George IV*, 1838, vol II, p 63.

52 George Wilson, *Healthy Life and Healthy Dwellings*, 1880, p 172.

53 Thomas Landseer, op cit, pp 39–40.

54 Allan Cunningham, op cit, vol II, p 333.

55 Ibid, vol III, p 67.

56 *The Times*, 18 January 1833.

57 Mrs Frank Russell, *Fragments of Auld Lang Syne*, no date, p 206.

58 Quoted in Archie Nathan, *Costumes by Nathan*, 1960, p 59.

59 Quoted in Hugh Tours, *Life and Letters of Emma Hamilton*, 1963, p 81.

60 Johann Wolfgang Goethe, *Italian Journey*, translated by W H Auden and Elizabeth Mayer, 1970, p 208.

61 Quoted in Owen Sherrard, *A Life of Emma Hamilton*, 1927, p 231.

62 Quoted in Hugh Tours, op cit, p 91.

63 John Thomas Smith, op cit, p 433.

64 Playbill for Cooke's Circus, no date, National Library of Scotland, R 283 C 26 no 35.

65 Edgar Yoxall Jones, *Father of Art Photography: O G Rejlander 1813–1875*, 1973, p 22.

66 Quoted in A M W Stirling, op cit, p 136.

67 Quoted in Helmut Gernsheim, *Julia Margaret Cameron*, 1975, p 75.

68 James Greig (editor), *The Diaries of a Duchess. Extracts from the Diaries of the First Duchess of Northumberland (1716–1776)*, 1926, pp 81–2, 93–4.

69 W Le Fanu (editor), *Betsy Sheridan's Journal*, 1960, p 168.

70 'Account for the King's Highland Accoutrements', manuscript in the Royal Archives at Windsor Castle, quoted in J N M Maclean and B Skinner, *The Royal Visit of 1822*, 1972.

71 Zillah Halls, *Coronation Costume 1685–1953*, 1973, catalogue nos 5, 7.

72 James Robinson Planché, *Souvenir of the Bal Costumé given by Her Most Gracious Majesty Queen Victoria at Buckingham Palace, May 12, 1842*, 1843, illustrated by F Coke Smyth.

73 Madeleine Ginsburg, 'The Young Queen and Her Clothes', *Early Victorian*, Proceedings of the Costume Society's Spring conference, 1969, pp 39–46.

74 It may have been the Prince Consort who was the originator of the idea for the statue which shows him in Roman dress and another with his wife in Saxon costume.

75 James Robinson Planché, *Recollections and Reflections*, 1872, pp 53–7.

76 *Illustrated London News*, 21 June 1851.

77 *The Times*, 23 July 1874.

78 *Illustrated London News*, 10 July 1897.

79 Johann Wolfgang Goethe, op cit, pp 452, 454.

80 William Hadley (editor), *The Letters of Horace Walpole*, 1926, p 15.

81 *The Gentleman's Magazine*, 15 January 1773.

82 *Edinburgh Evening Courant*, 20 and 25 February 1786.

83 Ibid, 25 February 1786.

84 Advertisement for 'Grand Masquerade', National Library of Scotland, R 283 C 26.

85 *The Times*, 3 January 1833.

86 *Spectator*, 16 March 1711.

87 W E K Anderson, *The Journal of Sir Walter Scott*, 1972, p 438.

88 Quoted in Constance Russell, *Three Generations of Fascinating Women*, 1904, p 113.

89 *Country Life*, 24 July 1897.

90 Quoted in William Whitley, op cit, p 262.

91 Sidney Gilpin, *Sam Bough*, 1905, p 177.

92 John Brown, 'Mystifications', *Horae Subsecivae*, 1908, vol III, pp 117–166.

93 Lady Elizabeth Eastlake, op cit (1852).

94 "Mlle Sans-Gêne", 'Notes from my Diary', *Country Life*, 10 July 1897.

95 Archie Nathan, op cit, pp 56–7.

96 *Illustrated London News*, 29 January 1887.

97 I am indebted to Miss Jane Tozer for identifying the source of the design.

98 The copy illustrated was used by Cranston and Elliot, an Edinburgh shop.

99 Jean Philippe Worth, *A Century of Fashion*, translated by Ruth Scott Miller, 1928, pp 131–2.

100 Ardern Holt, *Fancy Dresses Described*, 1882, p 9.

101 *The Observer of the Times*, 21 July 1821.

102 A list is given in Ian Anstruther, *The Knight and the Umbrella*, 1963, a full account and discussion of the Eglinton Tournament, to which I am considerably indebted.

103 Anon, *Account of the Tournament given at Vienna in honour of the Allied Sovereigns 20th November 1814*, no date.

104 Lady Sykes forms the focal point of the composition. Maclise became her lover and the discovery of the affair caused her husband to begin divorce proceedings in June 1838. See Richard Ormond, *Daniel Maclise 1806–1870*, 1972, catalogue no 43.

105 George Frederic Watts, op cit, p 151.

106 *The Times*, 16 April 1838.

107 Peter Buchan, *The Eglinton Tournament and Gentleman Unmasked*, 1840, p 63.

108 Ian Anstruther, op cit, p 152.

109 For a full description and illustration of this and a second outfit thought to have been worn for the banquet, see Margaret H Swain, 'The costumes and armour worn at the Eglinton Tournament, 1839', Scottish Arts Review, 12, 1970, pp 23–9.

110 James Aikman, *An account of the tournament at Eglinton*, 1839, illustrated by W Gordon.

111 Anon, *The Passage of Arms at Eglinton*, 1839, p 22.

112 James Aikman, op cit, p 7.

113 Ian Anstruther, op cit, p 160.

114 James Aikman, op cit, p 5.

115 According to *A full report of the Grand Tournament at Eglinton Castle*, the artists present included 'William Allan, Simson, Maclise, Bewick, Franklin, D O Hill, Nixon, Campbell, McPherson junior, Corbold, Macnee, McLure, Mr Dunbar from Sutherland and Co'.

116 Anon, *Guide to the Tournament at Eglinton Castle on 28th and 29th August 1839*, 1839.

117 Charles Mackay, *Through the Long Day or Memorials of a Literary Life during Half a Century*, 1887, vol I, p 69.

118 *Illustrated London News*, 10 June 1843.

119 Charles Mackay, op cit.

120 Peter Buchan, op cit, p 57.

Printed in Scotland for Her Majesty's Stationery Office by Bell & Bain Ltd, Glasgow
Dd. 591282/3814 K32 53-2069 6/78

BOOK 1: THE RESTLESS UNIVERSE

Course preface: *The Physical World*

Welcome to *The Physical World*. This book is the first in a series of eight that provide an introduction to the main ideas and applications of physics. The books have been planned, designed and edited by staff at the Open University, the United Kingdom's largest university and one of the world's major distance teaching institutions. The books are intended for self-study and therefore provide a greater degree of support than most other textbooks.

The titles of the eight books are:

1   The restless Universe
2   Describing motion
3   Predicting motion
4   Classical physics of matter

5   Static fields and potentials
6   Dynamic fields and waves
7   Quantum physics: an introduction
8   Quantum physics of matter

The Open University course S207 *The Physical World* includes a variety of learning materials apart from the texts, most notably multimedia and videos. Each of these media has an important role to play in the overall strategy of the course. They are *essential* for Open University students and will be referred to at various points in the text. However if you are not studying with the Open University, and do not have access to these additional media, the books can be read in isolation: they provide a coherent introduction to physics, independent of other resources.

The production of *The Physical World* was made possible by generous contributions of time and effort from many individuals at a variety of institutions. We gratefully acknowledge these contributions and thank all the contributors, some of whom are named in the list inside the front cover. All those who have been involved with the production of *The Physical World* hope that it will deepen your understanding of our remarkable Universe and its laws. We also hope that you will enjoy learning about physics, its applications and its cultural significance.

John Bolton   Alan Durrant   Robert Lambourne   Joy Manners   Andrew Norton

Academic Editors of *The Physical World*

Introduction to Book I

Studying physics will change you as a person. At least it should. In studying physics you will encounter some of the deepest and most far-reaching concepts that have ever entered human consciousness. Knowledge gathered over many centuries, that has been subjected to continuous scientific scrutiny, will be presented, along with its applications. Fact will follow fact, useful theory will succeed useful theory. Amidst this rich mix of information, newcomers to physics might not always appreciate how major discoveries have radically changed our attitude to ourselves, our natural environment, and our place in the Universe. In *The Physical World* we have tried to avoid intellectual overload, to ensure that you have sufficient time to appreciate the significance of each of the main ideas and applications of physics. We want your exposure to physics to change you, and we want you to be consciously aware of that change.

As part of that effort, this book gives a qualitative overview of some of the 'big ideas' of physics. Presenting ideas in this way, largely shorn of detail, and without much of the evidence that supports them, should help you to see the big picture and to appreciate some of the deep links that exist between different parts of physics. But this approach also has its dangers. It may obscure the fact that physics is more than a set of ideas about the world, more than a bunch of results: physics is also a *process*, a way of investigating the world based on experiment and observation. One of the biggest of all the 'big ideas' is that claims about the physical world must ultimately be tested by experiment and observation. Maintaining contact with the real world in this way is the guiding principle behind all scientific investigations, including those carried out by physicists.

Another important function of this book is to stress that physics is a cultural enterprise. All too often physics can have the appearance of being a collection of facts, theories, laws and techniques that have somehow emerged from nowhere. This, of course, is not the case. Throughout the ages, it has been the endeavour of individual men and women that has made possible the growth of science and the advancement of physics. This book attempts to emphasize the cultural aspect of physics by providing biographical information about some great physicists of the past. The coverage is neither fair nor complete, but it should remind you that physics is a human creation. Most physicists delight in tales of the struggles, foibles and achievements of their predecessors, and many feel that their understanding of physics is enhanced by knowing something of the paths (including the dead ends) that their intellectual forbears have trodden.

Do not expect to understand everything you read in this book. On the surface, we hope that it provides a coherent and interesting survey. But the more you think about some of the issues raised, the more puzzling they may seem. If, at the end of the book, you are left with questions as well as answers, that will be an excellent starting point for the rest of the course.

Open University students should leave the text at this point and use the multimedia package *Space and the Universe*. At the end of this activity you should return to this text.

A note on powers of ten and significant figures

Physics involves many quantities that may be very large or very small. When discussing such quantities it is convenient to use *powers of ten notation*. According to this notation

$$1\,000\,000 = 10^6 = \text{a million}$$

$$\frac{1}{1000} = 0.001 = 10^{-3} = \text{a thousandth.}$$

The small superscript attached to the ten is called a *power*. As illustrated by the above examples, a positive power indicates the number of zeros after the 1; a negative power indicates the number of zeros before the 1, including the zero before the decimal point.

A quantity is said to be written in *scientific notation* when its value is written as a number between 1 and 10, multiplied by 10 raised to some power, multiplied by an appropriate unit. For example, the diameter of the Earth is about 12 760 kilometres; in scientific notation this could be written 1.276×10^4 km. One advantage of scientific notation is that it allows us to indicate the precision claimed for a given quantity. Stating that the Earth's diameter is 1.276×10^4 km really only claims that the diameter is somewhere between 12 755 kilometres and 12 765 kilometres. Had we been confident that the Earth's diameter was 12 760 kilometres, to the nearest kilometre, we should have written 1.2760×10^4 km. The meaningful digits in a number are called **significant figures**. (Significant figures do not include any zeros to the left of the first non-zero digit, so 0.0025 has *two* significant figures, for example.) One advantage of writing numerical values in scientific notation is, therefore, that all the digits in the number that multiplies the power of ten are *significant* figures.

As the course progresses, we will introduce the units in which physical quantities are generally measured. For example, time is measured in seconds, length in metres, energy in joules and electric current in amperes. A detailed understanding of these units is not needed yet, and would make a rather dull start to the course. In the few places where units appear in this book, please skip past them if the meaning is unclear.

Many physical quantities span vast ranges of magnitude. Figures 0.1 and 0.2 use images to indicate the range of lengths and times that are of importance in physics.

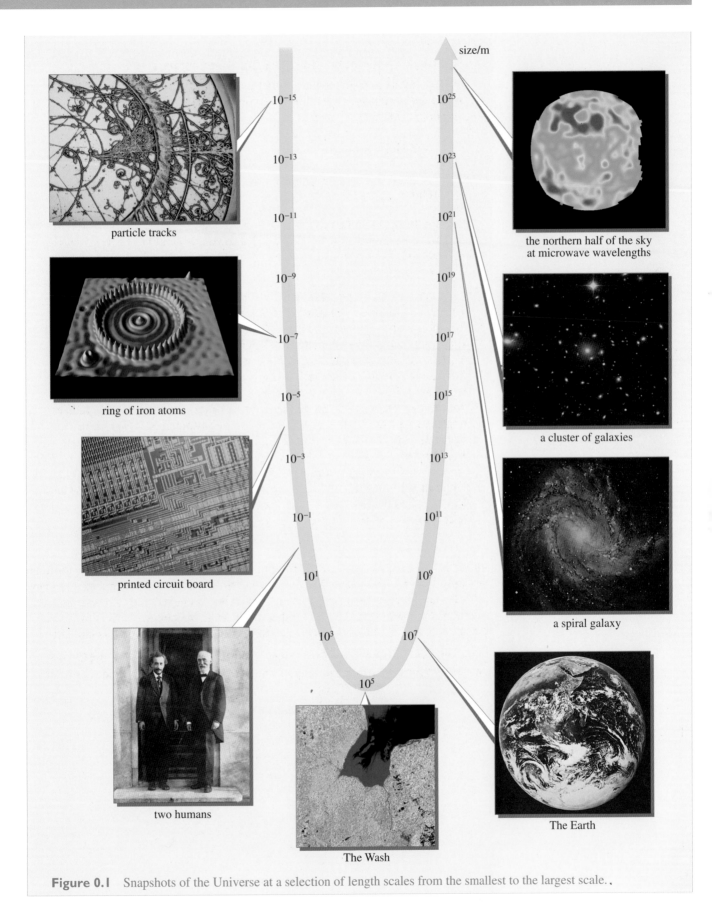

size/m

10^{-15}

10^{-13}

10^{-11}

10^{-9}

10^{-7}

10^{-5}

10^{-3}

10^{-1}

10^{1}

10^{3}

10^{5}

10^{25}

10^{23}

10^{21}

10^{19}

10^{17}

10^{15}

10^{13}

10^{11}

10^{9}

10^{7}

particle tracks

ring of iron atoms

printed circuit board

two humans

The Wash

the northern half of the sky
at microwave wavelengths

a cluster of galaxies

a spiral galaxy

The Earth

Figure 0.1   Snapshots of the Universe at a selection of length scales from the smallest to the largest scale.

Figure 0.2 A range of time scales of relevance to the Universe. Time is measured in billions of years since the Big Bang. The evolution of the Universe is marked by the onset of various ages: from the appearance of particles and galaxies to the emergence of life and intelligence.

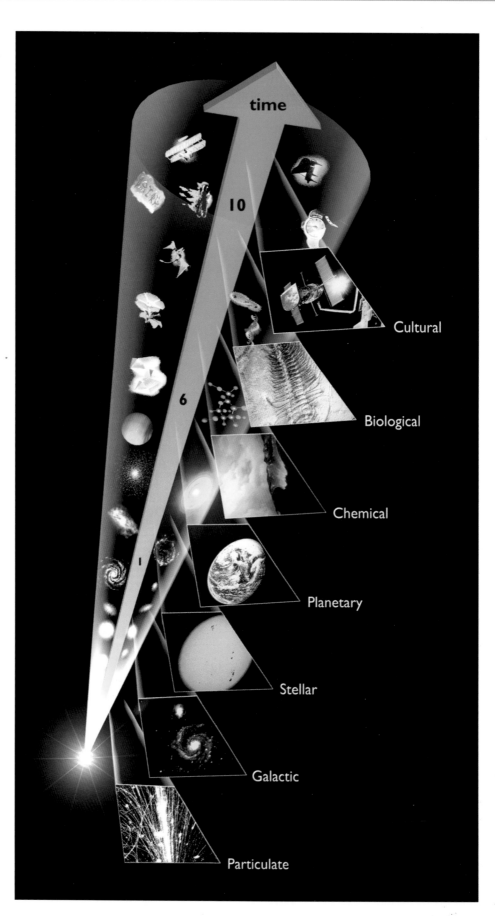

World-views

1 The lawful Universe

1.1 Science and regularity

'Our experience shows that only a small part of the physical Universe needs to be studied in order to elucidate its underlying themes and patterns of behaviour. At root this is what it means for there to exist laws of Nature, and it is why they are invaluable to us. They may allow an understanding of the whole Universe to be built up from the study of small selected parts of it.'

John D. Barrow (1988), *The World Within the World*, Oxford.

Science, it is widely agreed, originated from two main sources. One was the need to develop practical knowledge and to pass it from generation to generation. The other was a more spiritual concern with the nature and origin of the world. Common to both of these well-springs of science was an appreciation of the regularity of Nature. The way to build an arch that would not fall down today was to build it in much the same way as an arch that had not fallen down yesterday. The way to predict the waxing and waning of the Moon this month was to assume that it would follow much the same course as the waxing and waning that had been observed last month and the month before.

The observation of regularity in Nature allows *predictions* to be made concerning the future course of particular events. In many primitive societies these regularities were ascribed to the activities of gods or other mystical spirits. However, gradually, over a long period of time, there emerged the notion that the behaviour of the world was guided by a set of *natural laws* that were themselves regular, in the sense that identical situations could be expected to have identical outcomes.

One of the first scientists to make frequent use of the concept of a law of Nature, in the sense that we now use that term, was the Franciscan friar and scholar Roger Bacon (*c.* 1214–1292). Bacon is traditionally credited with the invention of the magnifying glass, but he is best remembered as an effective advocate of the *scientific method* and a follower of the maxim 'Cease to be ruled by dogmas and authorities; look at the world!' He lived at a time when the commonly accepted view of the world was fundamentally religious, and the Catholic church to which he belonged was coming to embrace the authority of the ancient Greek philosopher Aristotle on matters pertaining to physics and astronomy. Bacon's independence of mind brought him into conflict with the church, and he suffered fifteen years of imprisonment for heresy. Nonetheless, he helped to prepare the way for those who, irrespective of their own religious beliefs, insisted that the scientific investigation of Nature should be rooted in experiment and conducted on a purely rational basis, without reference to dogmatic authority.

Laws of Nature are now a central part of science. Carefully defined concepts, often expressed in mathematical terms, are related by natural laws which are themselves often expressed in a mathematical form. Just what those laws are is a central concern of physicists, who see their branch of science as the one most directly concerned with discovering and applying the fundamental laws of Nature. Improvements in our knowledge of natural laws have repeatedly led to a broadening and a deepening of our understanding of the physical world and hence to a change in the scientific world-view. However, the fundamental requirement that the laws should be rational and rooted in experiment has survived all changes to the detailed content of those laws.

Figure 1.1 Roger Bacon.

1.2 Mathematics and quantification

Roger Bacon once said 'Mathematics is the door and the key to the sciences'. This statement aptly summarizes the role of mathematics in science, particularly in physics, and it is not hard to see why.

Much of physics is concerned with things that can be measured and quantified, that is, expressed as numbers, multiplied by an appropriate unit of measurement such as a metre or a second. It is natural to turn to mathematics to try to reveal patterns underlying such measured data. This is more than a matter of arithmetic. By Roger Bacon's time the basic ideas of *algebra* had been developed, mainly by Arabic mathematicians and astronomers. The idea of *representing* a quantity by a symbol, such as x or t is extremely powerful because it allows us to express general relationships in a very compact way. For example, in the equation

$$h = \tfrac{1}{2} gt^2, \tag{1.1}$$

the symbol h represents the height fallen by an object that has been dropped from rest, the symbol t represents the time the object has been falling, and g is a constant with a known value ($g = 9.81$ metres per second per second). Equation 1.1 encapsulates a wealth of information about falling objects, information that is precise and useful. The tools of algebra allow us to go further. For example, the above equation can be rearranged to read

$$t = \sqrt{\frac{2h}{g}}, \tag{1.2}$$

so now, if we know the height fallen by an object, we can work out how long it has taken to fall.

Mathematics provides a natural medium for rational argument. Given an equation that relates various quantities, the rules of mathematics allow that equation to be re-expressed in a number of different but logically equivalent ways, all of which are valid if the original equation was valid. Given two equations, mathematical reasoning allows them to be combined to produce new equations which are again valid if the original equations were valid. Long chains of reasoning can be put together in this way, all of which are guaranteed to be correct provided that the starting points are correct and no mathematical rules are transgressed. Quite often these arguments are so long and detailed that it would be impossible to follow them in ordinary language, even if it were possible to express them at all.

Mathematics has been an immensely effective part of the scientist's toolkit throughout history. It was the increased use of mathematics in the sixteenth and seventeenth centuries, in the hands of individuals such as Galileo Galilei (1564–1642) and Isaac Newton (1642–1727), that opened a new era of physics and marked one of the greatest flowerings of science. Galileo and Newton, it should be noted, were both, at key times in their careers, professors of mathematics. In both cases they brought mathematical precision and rigour to the study of science, and in Newton's case made major breakthroughs in mathematics in the process. The types of mathematics used in physics are extremely varied. Practically every branch of mathematics that has developed over the centuries has been used within physics. Sometimes physics has provided direct inspiration for new mathematical concepts, sometimes abstract mathematical theories have found completely unexpected uses in physics, years after their introduction as products of pure thought.

Despite its power, physics students often find the extensive use of mathematics troublesome and some think of mathematics as providing a barrier to understanding. Do not let this happen to you. From the outset, you should regard mathematics as a friend rather than a foe. As the course progresses, you may meet some mathematical ideas that are new to you, or you may need to improve your ability to use methods you have met before. These are not distractions from trying to understand physics, but are the tools needed to make that understanding possible. It is only through using mathematics that a secure understanding can be achieved. When you see an equation, welcome its concision and clarity and try to 'read' the equation just as you would the large number of words it replaces. Learn to get beneath the squiggles and the equals sign and to understand the quantitative assertion that is being made.

Figure 1.2 "I see through your squiggles."

Later, you will see how graphs can be used to visualize an equation and how consideration of special cases and trends can help unpack its meaning.

Question 1.1 When Jesuits first visited China they spoke about the 'laws of science'. The Chinese thought this was a ridiculous notion: people could be persuaded to obey the laws of the Emperor, but sticks and stones have no intelligence so it is absurd to think of them as 'obeying laws'. How would you respond to this? ■

2 The clockwork Universe

2.1 Mechanics and determinism

It is probably fair to say that no single individual has had a greater influence on the scientific view of the world than Isaac Newton. The main reason for Newton's prominence was his own intrinsic genius, but another important factor was the particular state of knowledge when he was, in his own phrase, 'in the prime of my age for invention'.

In 1543, a century before Newton's birth, Nicolaus Copernicus launched a scientific revolution by rejecting the prevailing Earth-centred view of the Universe in favour

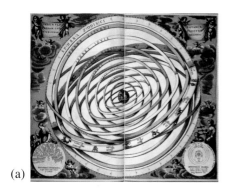  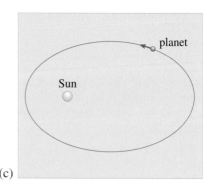

(a)　　　　　　　　　　(b)　　　　　　　　　　(c)

Figure 1.3　Three views of planetary motion. (a) The Earth-centred view of the ancient Greeks and of the Catholic church in the sixteenth century. (b) The Copernican system, in which the planets move in collections of circles around the Sun. (c) The Keplerian system in which a planet follows an elliptical orbit, with the Sun at one focus of the ellipse.

of a **heliocentric** view in which the Earth moved round the Sun. By removing the Earth, and with it humankind, from the centre of creation, Copernicus had set the scene for a number of confrontations between the Catholic church and some of its more independently minded followers. The most famous of these must surely have been Galileo, who was summoned to appear before the Inquisition in 1633, on a charge of heresy, for supporting Copernicus' ideas. As a result Galileo was 'shown the instruments of torture', and invited to renounce his declared opinion that the Earth moves around the Sun. This he did, though tradition has it that at the end of his renunciation he muttered '*Eppur si muove*' ('And yet it moves').

In the Protestant countries of Northern Europe, thought on astronomical matters was more free, and it was there in the early seventeenth century, that the German-born astronomer Johannes Kepler (1571–1630) devised a modified form of Copernicanism that was in good agreement with the best observational data available at the time. According to Kepler, the planets *did* move around the Sun, but their orbital paths were ellipses rather than collections of circles. This discovery, first published in 1609 in Kepler's book *Astronomia Nova* (The New Astronomy), was essentially an observational result. Kepler had no real reason to *expect* that the planets would move in ellipses, though he did speculate that they might be impelled by some kind of magnetic influence emanating from the Sun.

Kepler's ideas were underpinned by new discoveries in mathematics. Chief among these was the realization, by René Descartes, that problems in geometry can be recast as problems in algebra. Like most revolutionary ideas, the concept is disarmingly simple. Imagine a giant grid extending over the whole of space. Figure 1.4 shows the two-dimensional case, with a grid extending over part of the page. The grid is calibrated (in centimetres) so the position of any point can be specified by giving its x- and y-coordinates on the grid. For example, the coordinates of point A are $x = 3$ cm and $y = 4$ cm.

This idea becomes more powerful when we consider lines and geometrical shapes. The straight line shown in Figure 1.5 is characterized by the fact that, at each point along the line, the y-coordinate is half the x-coordinate. Thus, the x- and y- coordinates of each point on the line obey the equation $y = 0.5x$, and this is said to be the equation of the

line. Similarly, the circle in Figure 1.5 is characterized by the equation $\sqrt{x^2 + y^2} = 2$ cm. This is the beginning of a branch of mathematics, called *coordinate geometry*, which represents geometrical shapes by equations, and which establishes geometrical truths by combining and rearranging those equations. Sometimes, what is difficult to show using traditional geometry is easy to establish using algebra, so this 'mapping' of geometry into algebra gave scientists new ways of tackling geometrical problems, allowing them to go further than the greatest mathematicians of ancient Greece.

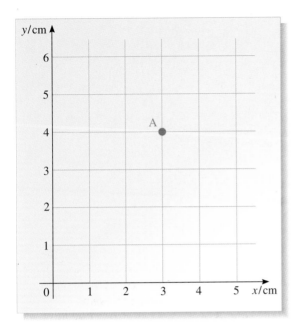

Figure 1.4 A two-dimensional coordinate system can be used to locate the position of any point in terms of its *x*- and *y*-coordinates.

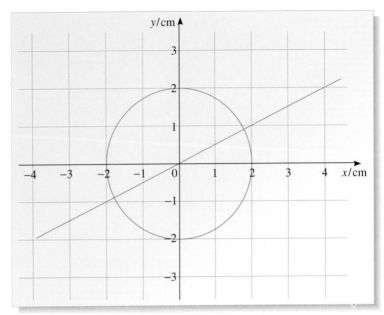

Figure 1.5 A two-dimensional coordinate system can be used to represent lines and other geometrical shapes by equations.

Newton's good fortune was to be active in physics (or 'natural philosophy' as it would then have been called) at a time when the cause of Kepler's ellipses was still unexplained and the tools of geometry were ripe for exploitation. The physics of Aristotle was clearly inadequate, and all other attempts seemed unconvincing. The new astronomy called for a new physics which Newton had the ability and the opportunity to devise. He was the right man, in the right place, at the right time.

Isaac Newton (1642–1727)

Isaac Newton was born on Christmas Day 1642 at Woolsthorp in Lincolnshire, England. His father had died a few months before the birth and Newton himself was born so prematurely that it was thought he might not survive. Newton was partly brought up by his grandmother, and seems not to have had a close relationship with his mother. He exhibited no great talent at school, but managed to avoid the task of managing his mother's farmlands and became instead an undergraduate at Trinity College in the University of Cambridge.

As a student Newton read the works of Aristotle and was taught mathematics, as was customary, but he also taught himself physics and thus became acquainted with the works of Galileo and Kepler, amongst others. He graduated in 1665, by which time he had already started to break new ground in mathematics. Due to an outbreak of plague, the University of Cambridge was closed for much of the next two years and Newton spent most of his time back at Woolsthorp. It was during this period that he made many of his greatest breakthroughs, or at least laid their foundations. Over an eighteen month period he:

- made fundamental advances in mathematics (essentially creating the subject of *calculus*, which has become a major part of the language of physics);
- used a glass prism to demonstrate that white light is actually a mixture of colours;
- began to consider the possibility that gravity, which obviously influenced bodies close to the Earth, might be a universal phenomenon holding the Moon in its orbit around the Earth and the Earth in its orbit around the Sun.

Following the reopening of the University, Newton returned to Trinity College where he became a Fellow in 1667. Two years later, still only 26, he was appointed Lucasian Professor of Mathematics on the recommendation of his predecessor, Isaac Barrow.

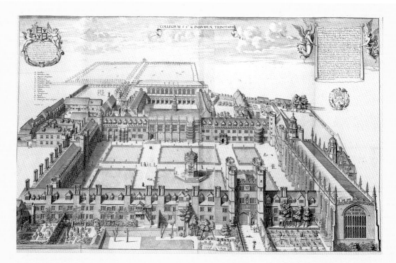

Figure 1.8 Trinity College, Cambridge around 1690.

Figure 1.6 Isaac Newton.

Figure 1.7 Woolsthorp Manor —
Newton's birthplace.

In addition to combining mathematical genius and profound physical insight, Newton also possessed practical skills. He built the furnaces in his own small laboratory in Trinity College, where he personally carried out alchemical experiments. He also constructed a novel kind of reflecting telescope, for which he was elected a Fellow of the Royal Society. However, Newton was a solitary and difficult person who has often been described as neurotic. He reacted badly to criticism and expected to get full credit for his discoveries even though he often did little to publicize them. He became involved in a number of bitter disputes over priority. Newton also harboured unconventional religious views (he was essentially a Unitarian) which prevented him from becoming the Master of his college. In 1678 he apparently suffered a nervous breakdown and for several years thereafter concentrated on alchemy and scriptural studies.

Newton was recalled to natural philosophy in 1684 by the young astronomer Edmond Halley who asked how a planet would move if it was attracted towards the Sun by a force that weakened in proportion to the inverse square of its distance from the Sun: in symbols, force $\propto 1/(\text{distance})^2$. (This means, for example, that increasing the distance by a factor of three decreases the force by a factor of *nine*.) Newton is said to have immediately told Halley the answer (an ellipse) having worked it out during the plague years. Halley persuaded Newton to recreate his calculations and publish them. The result, in 1686, was what is widely regarded as the most influential book in the history of science, Newton's *Philosophiae Naturalis Principia Mathematica* (Mathematical Principles of Natural Philosophy), a work usually referred to simply as *Principia*. In the opening pages of this book, Newton presented his definitions of force and mass, and his three laws of motion. He then went on to demonstrate that a body attracted towards a fixed point by a force that varied in proportion to the inverse square of its distance from that point would, in many circumstances, follow an elliptical path. After establishing many other results Newton presented, in Part 3 of the book, his *System of the World* in which he proposed that gravity was a universal force, acting between *any* two particles of matter, with a magnitude that is proportional to the product of their masses and the inverse square of their separation — just the kind of inverse square law that Halley had asked about. Thus Newton was able to explain the observed motion of the planets. He went on to consider the Moon's motion in detail (taking account of the gravitational influence of both the Earth and the Sun), the behaviour of comets, and the gravitational origin of the Earth's oceanic tides. The scope and power of *Principia* caused a sensation, and made Newton the foremost scientist of his time, or perhaps any time.

Newton suffered another breakdown in 1693 and subsequently quit Cambridge and the academic life in favour of London and the world of affairs. He became Warden of the Mint in 1696 and successfully oversaw the introduction of a new coinage. As a consequence he was appointed to a lucrative position as Master of the Mint and devoted much of his remaining time to theology and biblical chronology. He was elected President of the Royal Society in 1703, published his last great scientific work *Opticks* in 1704 (based on work performed many years earlier), and was knighted in 1705. He died, in London in 1727, and is buried in Westminster Abbey.

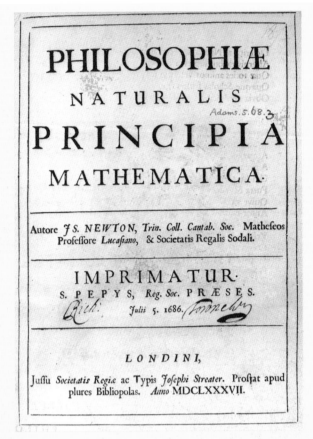

Figure I.9 *Principia* — Newton's masterpiece.

For years before Newton, people had been trying to understand the world from a scientific perspective, discovering laws that would help explain why things happen in the way that they do. Bits of knowledge were assembled, but there was no clear idea how these bits related to one another; understanding was fragmentary. Newton's great achievement was to provide a synthesis of scientific knowledge. He did not claim to have all the answers, but he discovered a convincing quantitative framework that seemed to underlie everything else. For the first time, scientists felt they understood the fundamentals, and it seemed that future advances would merely fill in the details of Newton's grand vision. Before Newton, few could have imagined that such a world-view would be possible. Later generations looked back with envy at Newton's good fortune. As the great Italian–French scientist Joseph Lagrange remarked:

'There is only one Universe … It can happen to only one man in the world's history to be the interpreter of its laws.'

At the core of Newton's world-view is the belief that all the motion we see around us can be explained in terms of a single set of laws. We cannot give the details of these laws now, but it is appropriate to mention three key points:

1   Newton concentrated not so much on motion, as on *deviation from steady motion* — deviation that occurs, for example, when an object speeds up, or slows down, or veers off in a new direction.

2   Wherever deviation from steady motion occurred, Newton looked for a cause. Slowing down, for example, might be caused by braking. He described such a cause as a force. We are all familiar with the idea of applying a force, whenever we use our muscles to push or pull anything.

3   Finally Newton produced a quantitative link between force and deviation from steady motion and, at least in the case of gravity, quantified the force by proposing his famous law of universal gravitation.

In keeping with his grand vision, Newton proposed just one law for gravity — a law that worked for every scrap of matter in the Universe, for moons and planets as well as for apples and the Earth. By combining this law with his general laws of motion, Newton was able to demonstrate mathematically that a single planet would move around the Sun in an elliptical orbit, just as Kepler claimed each of the planets did. Moreover, thanks to the understanding that gravity was the cause of planetary motion, Newtonian physics was able to predict that gravitational attractions between the planets would cause small departures from the purely elliptical motion that Kepler had described. In this way, Newton was able to explain Kepler's results and to go beyond them.

Books 2 and 3 give a thorough discussion of mechanics.

In the hands of Newton's successors, notably the French scientist Pierre Simon Laplace (1749–1827), Newton's discoveries became the basis for a detailed and comprehensive study of **mechanics** (the study of force and motion). The upshot of all this was a mechanical world-view that regarded the Universe as something that unfolded according to mathematical laws with all the precision and inevitability of a well-made clock. The detailed character of the Newtonian laws was such that once this majestic clockwork had been set in motion, its future development was, in principle, entirely predictable. This property of Newtonian mechanics is called **determinism**. It had an enormously important implication. Given an accurate description of the character, position and velocity of every particle in the Universe at some particular moment (i.e. the *initial condition* of the Universe), and an understanding of the forces that operated between those particles, the subsequent development of the Universe could be predicted with as much accuracy as desired.

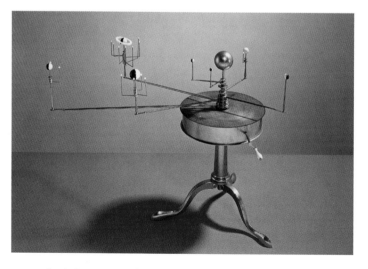

Figure 1.10 An orrery (a mechanical model of the Solar System) can be taken as a metaphor for the clockwork Universe of Newtonian mechanics.

Needless to say, obtaining a completely detailed description of the entire Universe at any one time was not a realistic undertaking, nor was solving all the equations required to predict its future course. But that wasn't the point. It was enough that the future was ordained. If you accepted the proposition that humans were entirely physical systems, composed of particles of matter obeying physical laws of motion, then in principle, every future human action would be already determined by the past. For some this was the ultimate indication of God: where there was a design there must be a Designer, where there was a clock there must have been a Clockmaker. For others it was just the opposite, a denial of the doctrine of **free will** which asserts that human beings are free to determine their own actions. Even for those without religious convictions, the notion that our every thought and action was pre-determined in principle, even if unpredictable in practice, made the Newtonian Universe seem strangely discordant with our everyday experience of the vagaries of human life.

Question 1.2   In principle, according to Newtonian mechanics, it is possible to predict the entire future behaviour of the Universe provided the initial positions and velocities of all the particles in it are known, and the laws describing their interactions are known. List at least two reasons why this goal is, in practice, beyond our reach.   ∎

2.2 Energy and conservation

Newtonian mechanics is concerned with explaining motion, yet it contains within it the much simpler idea that some things never change. Take the concept of mass, for example, which appears throughout Newtonian mechanics, including the law of gravitation. In Newtonian mechanics, mass is conserved. This means that the mass of the Universe is constant and the mass of any specified collection of particles is constant, no matter how much rearrangement occurs within the system. A chemist might take one kilogram of hydrogen and let it react with eight kilograms of oxygen to produce water. According to the **law of conservation of mass**, nine kilograms of water will be produced, the same as the total mass of the ingredients (1 kg + 8 kg = 9 kg). You may think this is trivial, but it is not. **Conservation laws** are rare and wonderful things. There is no general law of conservation of volume for example. The initial volume of the hydrogen and oxygen is far greater than the final volume of the water. The fact that mass is conserved really is a deep discovery about the checks and balances that exist in our Universe.

The conservation of energy is dealt with in detail in Book 3.

Newtonian mechanics introduced several other important conservation laws, including the celebrated **law of conservation of energy**. Not too surprisingly, this law states that the total energy of the Universe is constant and the total energy of an isolated system of particles is constant. But the full meaning of these words will only become apparent once the concept of energy has been properly defined.

For the moment, it is sufficient to note that we all have some familiarity with the concept of energy. We pay money for gas, electricity and petrol precisely because they are sources of energy, and we use that energy to heat and light our homes and to drive cars. From this, it is apparent that energy has many different forms — chemical energy in gas or electrical energy can be converted into light energy, thermal energy, or the energy of a whirring vacuum cleaner. It is possible to change energy from one form into another but, crucially, when all these forms are properly quantified, the total amount of energy remains constant. Energy is neither created or destroyed because it is a conserved quantity.

Perhaps the simplest form of energy is **kinetic energy**: the energy associated with motion. If a particle has mass m and speed v, its kinetic energy is given by the formula

$$E = \tfrac{1}{2}mv^2. \tag{1.3}$$

Suppose the particle hits a wall and is brought to a sudden halt. It then has no speed and no kinetic energy, but the initial energy has not been lost. Rather, it has been converted into other forms of energy, such as those associated with sound and heat.

The conservation of energy can be illustrated by considering a stone that is thrown vertically upwards. The stone starts out with a certain amount of kinetic energy, but as it climbs it slows down and its kinetic energy decreases. What happens to this energy? The answer is that there is another form of energy called **potential energy**, which in this case is associated with the downward pull of gravity and increases as the stone climbs. On the upward part of its journey, the stone's kinetic energy is gradually converted into potential energy until, at the top of its flight, the stone is momentarily at rest. At this point, the stone has no kinetic energy and its potential energy is at its highest. On the way down, potential energy is converted back into kinetic energy, as the stone loses height and gains speed. Assuming that no other forms of energy are involved, by the time the stone returns to its initial height, all of its initial kinetic energy is recovered and the stone is once again travelling at its initial speed. Figure 1.11 shows how the kinetic and potential energies of the stone vary during its up-and-down flight. The total energy, formed by adding the kinetic and potential energies together, is also shown. You can see quite clearly that energy is converted from one form to another while the total energy remains fixed.

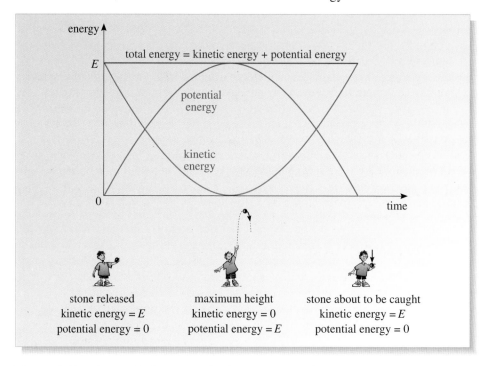

Figure 1.11 A stone is thrown vertically upwards and falls down again. The graph shows how the kinetic energy, potential energy and total energy vary as a stone travels up and down again. (For convenience, the potential energy is taken to be zero when the stone is launched, and when it is caught again.)

One of the consequences of the conservation of energy is that it makes sense to think of storing energy in order to have a ready supply whenever required. Figure 1.12 shows several examples of energy storage in action.

(a)

(b)

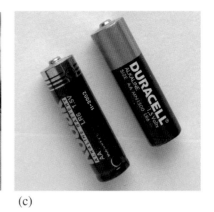
(c)

Figure 1.12 Some examples of energy storage. (a) A hydroelectric scheme in which the gravitational potential energy of water descending from a high lake is used to drive generators that produce electricity. (b) Petrol, a liquid from which it is easy to extract chemical energy. (c) An electrical dry cell which stores electrical energy.

3   The irreversible Universe

'Science owes more to the steam engine than the steam engine owes to Science.'

L. J. Henderson (1917)

From the time of Newton till the end of the nineteenth century the development of physics consisted essentially of the refinement and extension of the mechanical view of the Universe. There were many stages in this process but one of the most interesting came towards its end with the realization that the cosmic clockwork was inevitably unwinding and running down. The source of this realization was the development of thermodynamics.

3.1 Thermodynamics and entropy

The first half of the nineteenth century was a period of great economic and industrial growth. The steam engine, invented in the previous century, was becoming increasingly common in locomotives, mines and factories; power was becoming available on demand. A major priority for engineers was to produce more efficient engines, in order to deliver more useful power for less expenditure on fuel. **Thermodynamics** emerged as a study of the basic principles determining energy flows and the efficiency of machines.

This may seem like a big idea in engineering rather than a big idea in physics. Certainly, thermodynamics is important to engineers, and continues to guide the design of engines of all sorts, but thermodynamics is just as important to physicists. It explains a wealth of natural phenomena, from the freezing of water to the evaporation of a black hole, and casts light on concepts like temperature, heat and spontaneous processes, which do not fit naturally into the Newtonian world-view.

It is still instructive to return to the origins of the subject. Speaking very roughly, a steam engine is a device which uses fuel to convert water into steam and uses the resulting expansion in volume to drive a piston. The kinetic energy of the piston is exploited using a variety of mechanical devices — gears, drive belts, camshafts and so on, but thermodynamics concentrates on the early stages of the process, where heat is used to create kinetic energy.

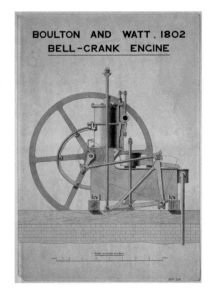

Figure 1.13 A steam engine, in which energy stored in coal is used to create heat to vaporize water. The resulting increase in volume drives a piston, so allowing useful work to be done.

To begin with there was much dispute about the nature of heat. Many people thought of it as a sort of fluid which could flow from one body to another. Eventually, it became clear that no such fluid exists and that **heat** is best defined as energy transferred because of a temperature difference. This scientific definition of the word 'heat' is slightly different from everyday usage, so it may help to consider a specific example. Think of a hot steak (veggie-burger, if you prefer) resting on a cold plate. The steak cools down and the plate warms up as energy flows from the steak to the plate. The energy transferred in this way is called heat. By contrast, **work** is energy transferred by non-thermal means. For example, if you rub the plate vigorously with a cloth, the energy of the plate will increase and it will get slightly warmer. But, this energy transfer is not *caused* by a temperature difference between the plate and the cloth, so energy transferred by rubbing is classified as work rather than heat.

In general, the total energy gained by a system (such as the plate) is the sum of the heat *and* the work transferred to it. It is worth emphasizing that heat and work are not themselves properties of a system. We cannot examine a plate and deduce that it has received so much energy from heat and so much energy from work. All that counts is that the plate *has* a total amount of energy, and that any increase in this energy is the sum of the heat and work transferred to the plate. This understanding of heat, work and energy is incorporated in the first law of thermodynamics.

First law of thermodynamics
When all types of energy transfer, including work and heat, are taken into account, the energy of an isolated system remains constant.

From a modern perspective, we can see that this is just another way of stating the law of conservation of energy with the explicit recognition of heat as a quantity of energy to be included, alongside work, in any energy audit. Inventors should take note: an engine may convert energy from one form to another, but it cannot produce energy from nothing. The kinetic energy of the piston of a steam engine, for instance, has been paid for in advance by the heat transferred to the steam.

Given this modern understanding of heat as energy transferred in a particular way, you might wonder why we bother to distinguish between heat and work at all. The reason is that heat can be used to define another important quantity: **entropy**.

Book 4 will discuss heat, temperature and entropy.

We cannot define entropy properly in this introductory survey. In very broad terms you can think of entropy as a measure of 'disorder' — the random motion of molecules in steam corresponds to more disorder, and hence more entropy, than the more orderly motion of molecules in ice. Interestingly enough, there is a connection between entropy and heat: whenever heat is transferred to a body, the entropy of that body increases. In the simplest case, if a small amount of heat Q is transferred gently to a body, whilst the temperature of the body is T, the entropy of the body increases by Q/T.

The term entropy was deliberately chosen to be reminiscent of energy, though the differences between the two quantities are just as important as their similarities. Entropy and energy are similar in that an isolated body may be said to have a certain 'entropy content' just as it may be said to have a certain 'energy content'. However, while the first law of thermodynamics ensures that the energy of an isolated system is always conserved, the second law of thermodynamics makes a slightly weaker assertion about entropy:

Second law of thermodynamics
The total entropy of an isolated system cannot decrease; it may (and generally does) increase.

The requirement that the total entropy should not decrease has the effect of ruling out enormous numbers of processes that are perfectly consistent with energy conservation. When heat flows between a steak and a plate there is no violation of energy conservation; the energy lost by the steak is gained by the plate. However, conservation of energy does not explain why the heat always flows *from* the hot steak *to* the cold plate; this is where the second law of thermodynamics comes in. Suppose the steak is at temperature T, the plate is at a slightly lower temperature $0.95T$, and that a small amount of heat Q is transferred from the steak to the plate. Then the entropy of the steak decreases by Q/T while the entropy of the plate increases by $Q/0.95T$. It is easy to see that the entropy lost by the steak is smaller than the entropy gained by the plate, so the total entropy of the Universe has increased; this process is therefore consistent with the second law of thermodynamics. If, on the other hand, heat Q had flowed from the cold plate to the hot steak, the entropy lost by the plate ($Q/0.95T$) would have been greater than the entropy gained by the steak (Q/T), and the total entropy of the Universe would have decreased. This violates the second law of thermodynamics, so we can be sure that the process is impossible. Heat flow is said to be an *irreversible* process — you will never see heat flowing spontaneously from a cold body to a hotter one.

Whenever energy is transferred or transformed, the final entropy of the Universe must be at least as high as the initial entropy. This usually means that heat flows are required to ensure that the total entropy does not decrease. Inventors should again take note. In most engines, heat is an unwanted by-product: the real aim is to transfer energy as work, perhaps to propel a vehicle or lift a weight. Since part of the energy initially stored in the fuel is inevitably wasted as heat, only a fraction is left to do useful work. Thus, thermodynamics imposes fundamental limits on the *efficiency* of engines. Fortunately, it also suggests ways of increasing efficiency, explaining for example, why a diesel engine is likely to be more efficient than a petrol engine, a topic we will return to in Book 4.

Question 1.3 When a room-temperature object is placed in a refrigerator, heat flows out of the object and its entropy decreases. Indeed, the refrigerator may be said to be a device for sucking entropy out of warm objects. How can such a decrease in entropy be consistent with the second law of thermodynamics? ■

3.2 Equilibrium and irreversibility

As the science of thermodynamics developed beyond its industrial roots, two powerful ideas came to the fore — **equilibrium** and **irreversibility**. These ideas were already implicit in studies of heat. You have already seen that heat flow from a hot steak to a cold plate is an irreversible process. The effect of this process is to cool down the hot steak and warm up the cold plate, leading to a more uniform distribution of temperature. The heat transfer continues until a state of equilibrium is reached, characterized by a completely uniform temperature.

Understanding the conditions needed for equilibrium, and the irreversible processes that drive systems towards equilibrium, has deep consequences throughout the sciences. For example, under normal conditions, the equilibrium state of carbon is graphite, rather than diamond. Fortunately, the processes that restore equilibrium are very slow in this case, so diamonds do not perceptibly turn into graphite. But, under some rather extreme conditions, diamond is the equilibrium state rather than graphite, and this fact can be used to create new diamonds from soot. More generally, thermodynamics determines which states of matter are in equilibrium under any given set of conditions.

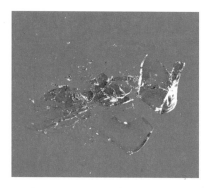

Figure 1.14 Some examples of irreversibility: (a) a smashed glass, (b) an omelette.

Entropy and the second law of thermodynamics provide the key to understanding equilibrium. An isolated system, free from all other influences, may undergo various spontaneous changes, some of which will increase its entropy. If the total entropy *increases* during a process, as it usually does, the process is irreversible — it is impossible to return to the starting point, leaving no other traces, since that would require a decrease in the total entropy, which is impossible. Once the entropy has increased, it cannot decrease again. An isolated system therefore approaches a state in which the entropy has the highest possible value. This is a state of equilibrium. In equilibrium, the entropy of the system cannot increase (because it is already at a maximum) and it cannot decrease (because that would violate the second law of thermodynamics). The only changes allowed are those in which the entropy remains constant. This equilibrium can be disturbed if the system is allowed to interact with its surroundings. The entropy of the system may then decrease, *provided* the entropy of the surroundings increases by at least as much, ensuring that there is no decrease in the entropy of the Universe as a whole.

If we start with a system that is close to, but has not quite reached, equilibrium, thermodynamics can suggest which processes will increase the entropy and lead towards equilibrium. Heat transfers are one source of entropy changes, but there are others. If you take two different gases and allow them to mix together in a flask that is so well insulated that no heat can be transferred to or from the flask, the entropy of the mixture turns out to be greater than the entropy of the two separate gases. That is why the mixing is an irreversible process. Once mixed, the gases will not spontaneously separate. Similar considerations explain why a dropped glass can shatter into a thousand fragments, but a thousand fragments will never spontaneously form themselves into a glass. Also, an egg can be made into an omelette, but an omelette will not make itself into an egg. There *is* an 'arrow of time' that points from the past to the future, and tomorrow *will* be different from today.

If these ideas are correct, the Universe must be inescapably and irreversibly approaching a state in which its entropy has the highest possible value. This will be a state of equilibrium for the Universe as a whole, where all the fuel will have been expended and the temperature will be uniform, leaving no prospect of generating heat flows and extracting useful work. In a phrase made popular in the 1930s by the Cambridge cosmologist Sir Arthur Eddington, the Universe is said to be approaching a final state of 'heat death'. In this sense, the clockwork of the Newtonian Universe is running down.

3.3 Statistical mechanics

You saw earlier that very strong claims were made for Newtonian mechanics. Many regarded it as a basic framework that would underlie all scientific explanations. It is therefore natural to ask about the relationship between Newtonian mechanics and thermodynamics:

- Do they contradict one another?
- Are they separate aspects of the truth?
- Can thermodynamics be derived from Newtonian mechanics?

These are not easy questions. Thermodynamics was specifically designed to deal with concepts like temperature, heat and entropy which had no clear Newtonian interpretation. The gulf between the two subjects can be illustrated by taking, say, a glass of water in a state of equilibrium. We now know that this contains an *enormous* number of molecules (roughly 10^{24}), each feeling electrical forces due to other molecules and moving rapidly around, colliding with other molecules in the liquid and the glass. The Newtonian world-view would require us to keep track of each and every molecule, building up an immensely complicated and detailed description. Of course, this is utterly beyond our powers. Even if it were possible, the results would provide little or no insight. It would be like looking at a painting under a microscope when its true significance is only apparent from a distance of a few metres. Thermodynamics adopts a more practical viewpoint. Rather than tracking each water molecule in detail, it uses just a few well-chosen variables — including energy, volume, pressure, temperature and entropy — to characterize the state of the water as a whole. The amazing thing is that this works. The thermodynamic description is massively incomplete, yet it is sufficient to make useful predictions.

There is a special branch of physics, called **statistical mechanics**, which attempts to bridge the gap between descriptions on the scale of molecules and thermodynamics. It recognizes that our knowledge of a complicated system, such as a glass of water, is inevitably incomplete so we are essentially reduced to making guesses. This may seem to be a terrible weakness, but statistical mechanics actually turns it into an advantage. It replaces precise knowledge of the motion of molecules by probabilities indicating how the molecules are likely to move, on average. It then goes on to estimate the probability of measuring a particular pressure, energy or entropy in the system as a whole. This is rather like the trick pulled by opinion pollsters when they predict the result of a general election without knowing how every individual in the country intends to vote. Pollsters have a mixed reputation, but the calculations of statistical mechanics are much more clear cut. They turn out to provide predictions that are *overwhelmingly* likely to happen — so much so, that they appear to be laws of Nature. The second law of thermodynamics is a case in point. From the viewpoint of statistical mechanics, the entropy of the Universe is not bound to increase, it is just overwhelmingly likely to do so. Perhaps 'heat death' will not be the end after all. After countless years of dull uniformity, a very unlikely (but possible) new fluctuation may occur with a lower than maximum entropy, and interesting things will start to happen again.

Figure 1.15 Ludwig Boltzmann (1844–1906).

Boltzmann, entropy and disorder

The statistical interpretation of thermodynamics was pioneered by James Clerk Maxwell (1831–1879) and brought to fruition by the Austrian physicist Ludwig Boltzmann.

In 1877 Boltzmann used statistical ideas to gain valuable insight into the meaning of entropy. He realized that entropy could be thought of as a measure of disorder, and that the second law of thermodynamics expressed the fact that disorder tends to increase. You have probably noticed this tendency in everyday life! However, you might also think that you have the power to step in, rearrange things a bit, and restore order. For example, you might decide to tidy up your wardrobe. Would this lead to a decrease in disorder, and hence a decrease in entropy? Actually, it would not. This is because there are inevitable side-effects: whilst sorting out your clothes, you will be breathing, metabolizing and warming your surroundings. When everything has been taken into account, the total disorder (as measured by the entropy) will have increased, in spite of the admirable state of order in your wardrobe. The second law of

thermodynamics is relentless. The total entropy and the total disorder are overwhelmingly unlikely to decrease.

Boltzmann's contribution was vital, but had a tragic outcome. Towards the end of the nineteenth century several puzzling facts (which eventually led to quantum theory), triggered a reaction against 'materialist' science, and some people even questioned whether atoms exist. Boltzmann, whose work was based on the concept of atoms, found himself cast as their chief defender and the debates became increasingly bitter. Always prone to bouts of depression, Boltzmann came to believe that his life's work had been rejected by the scientific community, although this was far from being true. In 1906, he committed suicide. If despair over rejection, or frustration over being unable to prove his point, were contributing factors the irony would be great indeed. Soon after Boltzmann's death, clinching evidence was found for atoms, and few would ever doubt their existence again.

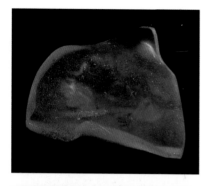

Figure 1.16 Examples of electric and magnetic forces. The ancient Greeks were aware that when samples of amber, which they called ηλεκτρον (electron), were rubbed with wool or fur they acquired the ability to attract light objects such as feathers. They were also aware that the substance we now call lodestone, which could be found in northern Greece in the area known as Magnesia, had the ability to attract pieces of iron.

Books 5 and 6 give a thorough discussion of electromagnetism.

4 The intangible Universe

4.1 Electromagnetism and fields

When Newton wrote about 'The System of the World' in Part 3 of *Principia*, the only forces he could discuss in any detail were the contact forces that arose when one object touched another, and gravity, which acted at a distance. Even so, Newton thought that there were other forces at work in the world, and hoped they might eventually be brought within his overall scheme just as gravity had been. In fact, Newton wrote:

> 'I wish we could derive the rest of the phenomena of Nature by the same kind of reasoning from mechanical principles, for I am induced by many reasons to suspect that they may all depend upon certain forces by which the particles of the bodies, by some causes hitherto unknown, are either mutually impelled towards one another, and cohere in regular figures, or are repelled and recede from one another.'

> Isaac Newton (1686), *Principia*.

Amongst the phenomena familiar to Newton, but which he could not treat mathematically, were those of *electricity* and *magnetism*, both of which had been known since antiquity (Figure 1.16). One of the key concepts that Newton lacked, but which eventually proved to be crucial to the quantification of both electricity and magnetism was that of *electric charge*. This was originally viewed as something like a fluid that could be passed from one object to another, but is now seen, rather like mass, as a fundamental attribute of matter. Just as Newton had been able to make gravity an effective part of the mechanistic world-view by declaring that the gravitational force between two point-like bodies was proportional to the product of their masses and the inverse square of their separation, so the French scientist Charles Coulomb (1736–1806) was able to do the same for electricity by showing that the electrical force between two point-like bodies was proportional to the product of their charges and the inverse square of their separation. In terms of symbols, this can be expressed as:

NEWTON	COULOMB
$F_{\text{grav}} \propto \dfrac{m_1 m_2}{r^2}$	$F_{\text{elec}} \propto \dfrac{q_1 q_2}{r^2}.$

However, electrical charge can be positive or negative, and the electrical forces can be attractive or repulsive in accordance with the famous dictum 'like charges repel; unlike charges attract'. Forces between magnets could be treated in a similar way by using north and south magnetic poles in place of positive and negative charges.

The incorporation of electrical and magnetic forces into the mechanistic world-view appeared to be a triumphant vindication of Newton's foresight. But it was really only the beginning of a story, not the end of one. Subsequent investigations were to show that an *electric* current — a flow of charge — could produce a *magnetic* force. This showed that the apparently separate subjects of electricity and magnetism were actually different aspects of a single subject: **electromagnetism**. It was within this unified subject that a new physical concept was to arise, that of a **field**. The field concept was destined to play an enormously important role in reshaping the physicist's view of the world. It would initially augment the mechanistic world-view, then around 1900, come to rival it, and ultimately, after 1926, play an important part in its downfall.

The field theory of electromagnetism was mainly the creation of two men, Michael Faraday and James Clerk Maxwell. They are, in a sense, the Galileo and the Newton of field theory.

Michael Faraday (1791–1867)

Michael Faraday was the son of a blacksmith. Apprenticed to a bookbinder at 14, he read about science, became enthralled with the subject, secured a job as a laboratory assistant at the Royal Institution in London, and eventually rose to be the Institution's Director and one of the most accomplished experimental researchers of all time. Amongst his many achievements, he is credited with the construction of the first electric motor and the discovery of both the principle and the method whereby a rotating magnet can be used to create an electric current in a coil of wire (still the basis of modern electricity generating plants). Faraday never became a very able mathematician, and it was his profoundly physical way of viewing the world that led him to create the concept of a field.

Figure 1.17 Michael Faraday.

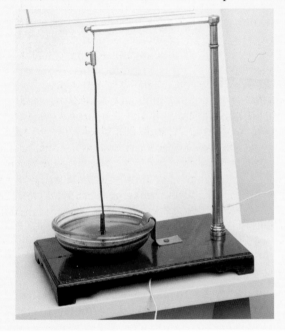

Figure 1.18 Faraday's apparatus demonstrating the principle of the electric motor. The upper end of a stiff wire is suspended in such a way that it is free to rotate. The lower end of the wire is immersed in the liquid metal mercury, and is free to move. The wire and its suspension form part of an electrical circuit that can be supplied with electric current from a battery. In the middle of the pool of mercury, next to the wire, is a short cylindrical magnet. When an electric current is passed through the wire it moves around the magnet. The use of mercury allows the current to continue flowing even though the wire is moving.

James Clerk Maxwell (1831–1879)

James Clerk Maxwell was the son of a Scottish laird. He studied at the Universities of Edinburgh and Cambridge and was appointed Professor of Natural Philosophy at Aberdeen at the age of 27. Four years later he moved to King's College, London, where he spent his most productive period. In 1865 he resigned his post in London but continued to work privately on his family estate in Scotland. In 1871 he agreed, somewhat reluctantly, to become the first Professor of Experimental Physics in the University of Cambridge. He died, from cancer, at the early age of 47, but by that time he had already made fundamental contributions to the theory of gases, the study of heat and thermodynamics, and, above all, to electromagnetism. He recast the discoveries of Faraday and others in mathematical form, added an important principle of his own and thus produced what are usually referred to as *Maxwell's equations* — the fundamental laws of electromagnetism (Figure 1.20). Much of his work on field theory was published in his masterpiece, *A Treatise on Electricity and Magnetism* (1873).

Figure 1.19 James Clerk Maxwell.

$$\text{div } \mathbf{D} = \rho_f$$

$$\text{div } \mathbf{B} = 0$$

$$\text{curl } \mathbf{E} = -\frac{\partial \mathbf{B}}{\partial t}$$

$$\text{curl } \mathbf{H} = \mathbf{j}_f + \frac{\partial \mathbf{D}}{\partial t}$$

Figure 1.20 Maxwell's equations, the fundamental laws of electromagnetism.

The problem that led Faraday to introduce the concept of a field was an old one; how could one body exert a force on another that was separated from it by empty space? Scientists and philosophers of earlier ages had devised essentially two possible answers.

● The simpler but less appealing possibility was that it just happened — that **action at a distance** was part of the fundamental reality of Nature and, as such, needed no further explanation.

● The other possibility was that the notion of empty space was a delusion, that the Universe was actually full of matter, albeit a very subtle and unusual form of matter, and that force was transmitted from one place to another by direct contact between parts of that matter. There were several different proposals concerning the exact nature of this 'subtle matter' that could transmit forces, but it was generally referred to as **ether**, and theories that made use of it were therefore called ether theories.

Newton's law of gravitation was taken to be an example of action at a distance. The law described the force that one body would exert on another some distance away without any regard to what was in between and without any hint of a mechanism for transmitting the force. Newton was aware that this was a feature of his 'System of the World' that many would find unattractive, but he also realized that he had no evidence on which to base a detailed explanation of gravitational forces. He contented himself with describing gravitational forces mathematically, and said in the *Principia*, that he would 'form no hypotheses' as to their cause.

Faraday, like others, was willing to accept this situation as far as a purely attractive force like gravity was concerned, or even for a force that could be attractive or repulsive like Coulomb's, but Faraday's own invention of the electric motor showed that the magnetic force on an electric current was not simply attractive or repulsive, it could cause rotation (see Figure 1.18). Faraday felt that for a wire to rotate around a magnet there had to be *something*, produced by the magnet but present at the location of the wire, that pushed the wire to one side rather than another. It was this agency, filling the space around the magnet, that Faraday eventually came to call a *magnetic field*.

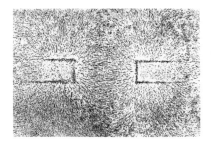

Figure 1.21 Magnetic field lines, as revealed by sprinkling iron filings onto a sheet of stiff paper placed on top of a magnet.

Faraday's views about the nature of the magnetic field changed over time; for complex reasons, he spoke about his field as being different from an ether. Whatever his precise views, Faraday was convinced that fields held the key to understanding magnetic and electrical phenomena. He certainly felt that the curved pattern of lines revealed by sprinkling iron filings onto a sheet of paper placed over a magnet (see Figure 1.21) showed the presence of a magnetic field. Like a collection of miniature compass needles, the filings showed the field's strength and direction in each region of space. However, he also realized that in order to provide *convincing* evidence of the reality of the field something more was needed, such as a demonstration that a disturbance at one point in the field would take a finite time to propagate through the field and have visible effects elsewhere. Faraday tried to observe such delays, but failed. Nevertheless, his belief in the physical reality of fields guided his experiments and lead him on to new discoveries.

When Maxwell started to work on electromagnetism he studied Faraday's experimental researches and, unlike most of his contemporaries, was impressed by the notion of a field. However, Maxwell had his own reasons for believing in an ether. In particular, he believed that an ether was necessary to account for the propagation of light, which was generally regarded as a kind of wavelike disturbance and was therefore thought to *require* a medium just as ocean waves require water. Maxwell therefore decided to combine Faraday's field ideas with the ether concept. He set out to treat electricity and magnetism in terms of fields that were themselves interpreted as manifestations of pressure, tension and motion within the ether.

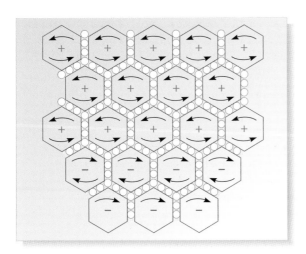

Figure 1.22 A part of Maxwell's mechanical model of the electromagnetic field. The model has been described as 'the most ingenious but least credible ever invented'.

In many ways, Maxwell was extraordinarily successful. He did formulate a mechanical model of the electromagnetic field (Figure 1.22) and used it as a guide in writing down his now famous equations. Amongst many other things, Maxwell's equations implied that light is a wave phenomenon in which electric and magnetic fields oscillate in space and time. In an astonishing demonstration of the power of these ideas, Maxwell took the fundamental constants of electricity and magnetism, entered them in his equations, and derived an accurate value for the speed of light. In this way, the subjects of electricity, magnetism and optics, which had seemed quite distinct at the beginning of the nineteenth century, were unified into a single branch of physics. The equations even led Maxwell to predict the existence of a wider family of electromagnetic waves, most with wavelengths beyond the range of human sight. In 1888 Heinrich Hertz completed a series of experiments which confirmed the existence of electromagnetic waves with wavelengths much greater than those of visible light. These were the radio waves which, within a few decades would transform both communication and entertainment. In 1895 Wilhelm Röntgen discovered X-rays, which proved to be electromagnetic waves with wavelengths much smaller than those of visible light. Yet, in spite of these successes, Maxwell's mechanical model of the electromagnetic field remained unconvincing. From about 1865, Maxwell himself drew a clear distinction between his equations, which described the behaviour of electric and magnetic fields, and the underlying ether mechanism that was supposed to account for them. Maxwell firmly believed that he had discovered the correct equations, but did not try to defend the model that had led to them.

If Maxwell had succeeded in accounting for the electromagnetic field in terms of motion in the ether, the mechanical world-view would have reigned supreme; but it was not to be. As investigations continued, particularly after Maxwell's untimely death, it became increasingly clear that it would be impossible to find a convincing mechanical basis for the electromagnetic field. On the other hand it also became clear that Maxwell's field theory of electromagnetism, as embodied in his equations, was stunningly successful.

Nowadays, with the scaffolding stripped away, we can recognize that the true achievement of Faraday and Maxwell was in establishing the importance of fields, arguably the most radical concept in physics since the time of Newton. We now know that there are many types of field: magnetic fields, electric fields, gravitational fields and so on. Each of these fields has a particular value at each point in space. The key idea is that a particle passing through a given point will experience forces that depend on the fields *at that point*, or in its immediate vicinity. This means that forces are determined locally — there is no action at a distance. When two particles interact they do so because one particle creates a field in the space around itself and the other particle then responds to this field. What is more, as Faraday anticipated and Maxwell's equations established, the fields have dynamics of their own, allowing disturbances of electric and magnetic fields to spread out as waves. Crucially, this means that fields should be thought of as *part of the fabric of the world* — more intangible than matter, but just as real. The electromagnetic field on Earth is incredibly complex. While you are reading this, electromagnetic waves from all the channels that your radio and television could possibly receive are passing straight through your head. Added to this are signals from power lines, domestic appliances, cars and the Big Bang; tiny electromagnetic signals are even reaching you from the brains of those around you. One of the attractions of physics is its ability to reveal a much richer world than is immediately apparent to our senses. And much stranger things are yet to come.

Question 1.4 Describe one way in which Maxwell's theory satisfied Faraday's desire to find evidence that disturbances at one point in the electromagnetic field would take a finite time to reach other points. ■

4.2 Relativity, space, time and gravity

Throughout the development of mechanics and electromagnetism, the role of space and time had been clear and simple. Space and time were simply the arena within which the drama of physics was played out. Speaking metaphorically, the principal 'actors' were matter and ether/fields; space and time provided the setting but didn't get involved in the action. All that changed with the advent of the theory of relativity.

The theory was developed in two parts. The first part is called the special theory of relativity, or, occasionally, the restricted theory, and was introduced in 1905. The second part is called the general theory, and dates from about 1916. Both parts were devised by the same man, Albert Einstein.

The special theory of relativity is discussed in Book 6.

The origins of the **special theory of relativity** can be traced back a long way. In 1632, Galileo wrote:

'Shut yourself up with some friend in the main cabin below decks on some large ship, and have with you there some flies, butterflies and other small flying animals. Have a large bowl of water with some fish in it; hang up a bottle that empties drop by drop into a wide vessel beneath it. With the ship standing still, observe carefully how the little animals fly with equal speed to all sides of the cabin. The fish swim indifferently in all directions; the drop falls into the vessel beneath; and, in throwing something to your friend, you need throw no more strongly in one direction than another, the distances being equal; jumping with your feet together, you pass equal spaces in every direction. When you have observed all these things carefully (though there is no doubt that when the ship is standing still everything must happen in this way), have the ship proceed with any speed you like, so long as the motion is uniform and not fluctuating this way and that. You will discover not the least change in all the effects named, nor could you tell from any of them whether the ship was moving or standing still.'

Galileo Galilei (1632), *Dialogue Concerning the Two Chief Systems of the World.*

In other words, any phenomenon you care to study occurs in just the same way in a steadily moving ship as in a stationary ship. The underlying physical laws and fundamental constants must therefore be exactly the same for all uniformly moving (or stationary) observers. This fact, which dozing train passengers may accept with gratitude, is the central idea of the theory of special relativity. Indeed, it is called the **principle of relativity**. This leaves one obvious question: how did Einstein gain both fame and notoriety for promoting an idea that was nearly three hundred years old?

The answer is that a lot of physics had been discovered between the time of Galileo and that of Einstein. Most notably Maxwell's theory of electromagnetism had achieved the feat of *predicting* the speed of light using fundamental constants of electromagnetism, constants that could be measured using simple laboratory equipment such as batteries, coils and meters. Now, if the principle of relativity were extended to cover Maxwell's theory, the fundamental constants of electromagnetism would be the same for all uniformly moving observers and a very strange conclusion would follow: all uniformly moving observers would measure the *same* speed of light. Someone running towards a torch would measure the same speed of light as someone running away from the torch. Who would give credence to such a possibility?

Einstein had the courage, self-confidence and determination to reassert the principle of relativity and accept the consequences. He realized that, if the speed of light were to remain the same for all uniformly moving observers, space and time would have to have unexpected properties, leading to a number of startling conclusions, including the following:

- *Moving clocks run slow*. If I move steadily past you, you will find that my wrist watch is ticking *slower* than yours. Our biological clocks are also ticking, and you will also find that I am ageing less rapidly than you.

- *Moving rods contract*. If an observer on a platform measures the length of a passing railway carriage, he or she will measure a *shorter* length than that measured by a passenger who is sitting inside the carriage.

- *Simultaneity is relative*. Suppose you find two bells in different church towers striking at exactly the same time (i.e. simultaneously). If I move steadily past you, I will find that they strike at different times (i.e. not simultaneously). It is even possible for you to find that some event A happens before some other event B and for me to find that they occur in the *opposite* order.

- *The speed of light in a vacuum is a fundamental speed limit*. It is impossible to accelerate any material object up to this speed.

If these consequences seem absurd, please suspend your disbelief. It took the genius of Einstein to realize that there was nothing illogical or contradictory in these statements, but that they describe the world as it is. Admittedly we don't notice these effects in everyday life but that is because we move slowly: relativistic effects only become significant at speeds comparable with the speed of light (2.998×10^8 metres per second). But not everything moves slowly. The electrons in the tube of a TV set are one example, found in most homes, where relativistic effects are significant.

One of the first people to embrace Einstein's ideas was his former teacher, Hermann Minkowski (1864–1909). He realized that although different observers experience the same events, they will *describe* them differently because they disagree about the nature of space and the nature of time. On the other hand space and time taken together form a more robust entity:

> 'Henceforth space by itself, and time by itself, are doomed to fade away into mere shadows, and only a kind of union of the two will preserve an independent reality.'
>
> Hermann Minkowski, *Space and Time* in A. Einstein et al. (1952), *The Principle of Relativity*, New York, Dover Publications.

The union of space and time of which Minkowski spoke is now generally referred to as *space-time*. It represents a kind of melding together of space and time, and since space is three-dimensional, and time is one-dimensional, space-time is four-dimensional. Any particular observer, such as you or I, will divide space-time into space and time, but the way in which that division is made may differ from one observer to another and will crucially depend on the relative motion of the observers.

A very rough attempt at representing diagrammatically this change of attitude towards space and time is shown in Figure 1.23. Before Einstein introduced special relativity, the phrase 'the whole of space at a particular time' was thought to have exactly the same meaning for all observers. After Einstein's work it was felt that each observer would understand what the phrase meant, but that different observers would *disagree* about what constituted the whole of space at a particular time. All observers would agree on what constituted space-time, but the way in which it was sliced up into space and time would differ from one observer to another, depending on their relative motion. No observer had the true view; they were all equally valid even though they might be different.

In retrospect, special relativity can be seen as part of a gradual process in which the laws of physics attained universal significance. The earliest attempts to understand the physical world placed Man and the Earth firmly at the centre of creation. Certain laws applied on Earth, but different laws applied in the heavens. Copernicus overturned this Earth-centred view and Newton proposed laws that claimed to apply at all places, and at all times. Special relativity continues this process by insisting that physical laws should not depend on the observer's state of motion — at least so long as that motion is uniform. It is therefore not surprising that Einstein was led to ask if physical laws could be expressed in the same way for *all* observers, even those who were moving *non-uniformly*. This was the aim of his **general theory of relativity**.

Einstein realized that many of the effects of non-uniform motion are similar to the effects of gravity. (Perhaps you have experienced the sensation of feeling heavier in a lift that is accelerating upwards.) With unerring instinct he treated this as a vital clue: any theory of general relativity would also have to be a theory of gravity. After more than ten years of struggle, the new theory was ready. According to general relativity, a large concentration of mass, such as the Earth, significantly distorts space-time in its vicinity. Bodies moving through a region of distorted space-time move differently from the way they would have moved in an undistorted space-time.

Figure 1.23 (a) The pre-Einsteinian view of space and time. Not only are space and time separate and distinct they are also absolute. All observers agree on what constitutes space and what constitutes time, and they also agree about what it means to speak of 'the whole of space at a particular time'. (b) The post-Einsteinian view in which space and time are seen as aspects of a unified space-time. Different observers in uniform, relative motion will each slice space-time into space and time, but they will do so in different ways. Each observer knows what it means to speak of 'the whole of space at a particular time', but different observers no longer necessarily agree about what constitutes space and what constitutes time.

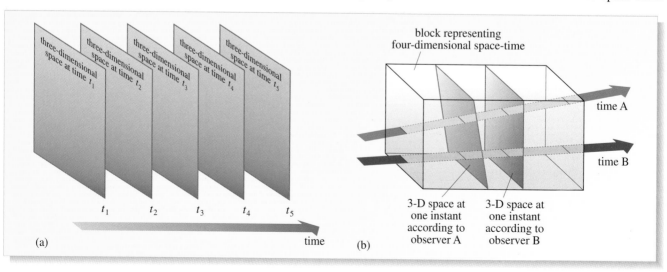

For example, meteors coming close to the Earth are attracted to it and deviate from uniform, steady motion in a straight line. Newton would have had no hesitation in saying that these deviations are due to gravitational forces. In Einstein's view, however, *there is no force*. The meteors move in the simplest way imaginable, but through a distorted space-time, and it is this distortion, generated by the presence of the Earth, that provides the attraction. This is the essence of general relativity, though the mathematics required to spell it out properly is quite formidable, even for a physicist.

The central ideas of general relativity have been neatly summarized by the American physicist John Archibald Wheeler. In a now famous phrase Wheeler said:

'Matter tells space how to curve.

Space tells matter how to move.'

Purists might quibble over whether Wheeler should have said 'space-time' rather than 'space', but as a two-line summary of general relativity this is hard to beat (see Figure 1.24). If you tried to summarize Newtonian gravitation in the same way all you could say is: 'Matter tells matter how to move'; the contrast is clear.

General relativity is a field theory of gravity. At its heart are a set of equations called the Einstein field equations. To this extent general relativity is similar to Maxwell's field theory of electromagnetism. But general relativity is a very unusual field theory. Whereas electric and magnetic fields exist *in* space and time, the gravitational field essentially *is* space and time. Einstein was well aware of the contrast between gravity and electromagnetism, and spent a good deal of the later part of his life trying to formulate a **unified field theory** in which gravity and electromagnetism would be combined into a single 'geometric' field theory. In this quest he was ultimately unsuccessful, but general relativity remains a monumental achievement.

> Open University students should leave the text at this point and view Video 1: *A Life of Time*. When you have viewed the video you should return to this text.

Question 1.5   Would it be fair to say that special relativity has the effect of leaving each observer completely free to make his or her own decision about what constitutes time?   ■

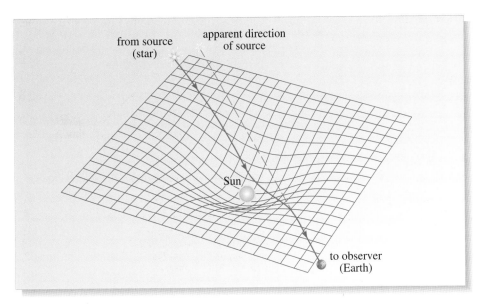

Figure 1.24   A highly schematic diagram showing space-time curvature near the Sun and indicating the way in which this can lead to the bending of starlight as it grazes the edge of the Sun. (The bending has been hugely exaggerated for the sake of clarity.) The observation of this effect in 1919, during a total eclipse of the Sun, did much to make Einstein an international celebrity.

Albert Einstein (1879–1955)

Figure 1.25 Albert Einstein.

Albert Einstein was born in Ulm, Germany on 14 March 1879. The following year he and his family moved to Munich where he had a successful, though not brilliant, school career. In 1896 Einstein renounced his German citizenship and started to study for a high-school teaching diploma at the prestigious Eidgenössische Technische Hochschule (ETH) in Zurich, Switzerland. Amongst his fellow students at ETH was Mileva Maric, who became his first wife. Einstein graduated in 1900 and in December of that year submitted his first paper to a scientific journal. However, he failed to get any of the university positions that he applied for, and after some temporary school teaching he became, in 1902, a technical expert (third-class) at the patent office in Bern. He continued to pursue his interest in physics while at the patent office, and worked on a doctoral thesis during his spare time.

1905 was an extraordinary year in Einstein's life and in the progress of science. During that year he produced four of his most important papers. In the first he explained Brownian motion — the apparently random motion exhibited by pollen grains and other small particles when they are suspended in a fluid. According to Einstein, the motion is a result of the incessant bombardment of the suspended particles by molecules of the fluid. The quantitative success of this explanation established beyond reasonable doubt the existence of molecules, which until then had been questioned by many physicists. In his second 1905 paper, Einstein formulated a theory of the

photoelectric effect — the liberation of electrons from a metal exposed to electromagnetic radiation. His explanation was one of the earliest applications of quantum physics and was an important step in the development of that subject. It was mainly for this piece of work that Einstein was awarded the Nobel Prize for Physics in 1921. His third and fourth 1905 papers concerned the special theory of relativity. He laid out the foundations of the subject in the third paper and in the fourth he provided a brief but eloquent justification of his famous equation $E = mc^2$, which uses c, the speed of light in a vacuum, to relate the mass m of a body to its total energy content E.

ON THE ELECTRODYNAMICS OF MOVING BODIES

BY

A. EINSTEIN

Translated from "Zur Elektrodynamik bewegter Körper," Annalen der Physik, 17, 1905.

Figure 1.26 Einstein's 1905 paper *On the Electrodynamics of Moving Bodies*. This was his first paper on special relativity.

Although these brilliantly original papers eventually established Einstein as a physicist of the first rank, three more years were to elapse before he obtained his first academic post. During that time he worked on a variety of topics and did pioneering work on the quantum physics of solids. In 1909 he was finally appointed to a lecturing post at the University of Bern, in 1911 he became a professor at the University of Prague and in 1912 he returned to Zurich, as Professor of Theoretical Physics at ETH. By this time his attention was focused on the search for a general theory of relativity that would extend his earlier work on the special theory. The principle of equivalence which he formulated in 1907 had convinced Einstein that a general theory of relativity would also be a new theory of gravity, and it was from the gravitational point of view that the problem of general relativity was attacked. In 1914 Einstein moved to Berlin, the main centre of scientific research in the German-speaking world, to take up a research professorship that would free him from teaching duties. He and his wife separated soon after the move, and were eventually divorced. Einstein continued to work on general relativity and in 1916 produced the first systematic treatment of the subject in a long paper entitled *Die Grundlage der allgemeinen Relativätstheorie* ('The foundations of general relativity theory'). The creation of general relativity was one of the greatest intellectual achievements of the twentieth century: it led on to the study of black holes and the prediction of gravitational waves, and it provided a firm basis for future investigations in cosmology — the study of the Universe as a whole. Observations carried out in 1919, during a total eclipse of the Sun, confirmed one of the key predictions of general relativity: the gravitational deflection of starlight passing close to the edge of the Sun. This quantitative success of Einstein's theory was widely reported, and did more than any other event to make Einstein into an instantly recognized icon of scientific genius.

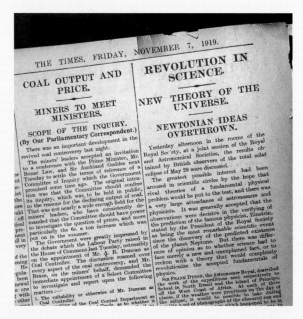

Figure 1.27 The article from the Times of November 7, 1919. Copyright Times Newspapers Limited, 1919.

Soon after completing the general theory, Einstein turned his attention to the quantum theory of electromagnetic radiation and postulated the existence of stimulated emission — the process that now underpins the operation of lasers. However, in 1917 he became seriously ill. He was nursed back to health by his cousin Elsa, whom he married in 1919. His second marriage seems to have been reasonably happy, but he was not, by his own admission, a good husband.

By the early 1920s Einstein's best scientific work was done: he wrote in 1921 'Discovery in the grand manner is for young people… and hence for me is a thing of the past'. He was none the less extremely influential in the physics community and he did much to prepare the ground for many later developments. He travelled a lot, and became increasingly active in social and political causes, particularly in support of Zionism. (Many years later he was offered the presidency of Israel, which he declined.) In 1932, Einstein and his wife left Germany for good, mainly in response to growing anti-Semitism, and moved to the USA where Einstein settled as a professor at the Institute for Advanced Study in Princeton, New Jersey. Einstein eventually became an American citizen, though he also retained the Swiss citizenship he had held since his twenties. Although Einstein was a believer in peace and harmony, and eventually argued for a world government, he also recognized the dangers of Nazism and the potential power of atomic science. As a result, in 1939, he was persuaded to co-sign a letter to the American President, Franklin D. Roosevelt, warning of the possibility of atomic weapons. This is widely thought to have had a decisive effect in prompting the US government to undertake the development of the atomic bomb, though Einstein himself played no part in the project.

Although Einstein had been deeply involved in the birth of quantum physics, he became increasingly dissatisfied with the way the subject developed after the mid-1920s. He did not believe that it gave a truly fundamental account of natural phenomena. His last major contribution to the field was the development of Bose–Einstein statistics in 1925. However his name is also recalled in the Einstein–Podolsky–Rosen experiment, a 'thought experiment' proposed in 1935 in an attempt to show that quantum physics was seriously flawed. The attempt was unconvincing, but it did emphasize the gulf that separated quantum physics from the classical physics that preceded it. The other project of Einstein's later years that continues to be remembered is his search for a unified field theory that would bring together gravity and electromagnetism. He continued to work on this up to the time of his death, often with great ingenuity, but little of that work is regarded as being of enduring value. He died in Princeton in 1955.

5   The uncertain Universe

Despite the impact of relativity, the greatest source of change in the scientific world-view in the twentieth century has undoubtedly been the development of *quantum physics*. This is the branch of physics that is mainly concerned with microscopic entities such as atoms and molecules, and their constituents. It is by far the most quantitatively accurate part of science, routinely providing predictions that are correct to just a few parts in a million. Quantum physics is also of enormous technological importance since it provides the scientific underpinning for the modern electronics industry which brings us devices ranging from TV sets and transistor radios to CD players and computers.

So great has been its effect that it is now conventional to divide physics into two parts; **quantum physics** and **classical physics**, where, by classical physics, we mean anything that is not quantum physics. To be fair, it should be noted that some authors prefer to define classical physics as consisting of those subjects that were already well-defined by the year 1900, together with their direct developments in the twentieth century. In this way they include mechanics, thermodynamics and electromagnetism, but they exclude special and general relativity. Most physicists, however, would not hesitate to say that general relativity was a classical theory of gravity, and would regard relativity as the culmination of classical physics rather than a step beyond it. In any event, there can be no doubt that the development of quantum physics has demanded a fundamental change in outlook by physicists.

Quantum physics was born in 1900, but it took about twenty five years to reach maturity. During the first quarter of the twentieth century it had a rather rickety feel; there was not really any coherent theory of quantum physics, just assorted quantum ideas that were so successful in solving certain outstanding puzzles that it seemed there had to be something behind it all. The strongest characteristic of quantum physics during this early period was an emphasis on graininess or discreteness.

Indeed, the word *quantum* actually comes from the Latin for 'unit of quantity' or 'amount' and was introduced into physics by the German scientist Max Planck (1858–1947), in the course of his investigations into the emission of electromagnetic radiation from hot surfaces.

Crudely speaking, Planck was looking into why hot things glow. He knew that the light given off by a heated object is a mixture of all the possible colours of light and he wanted to predict the relative brightness with which each colour would be emitted

Figure 1.28   The changing colour of a heated body. The emitted light is a mixture of colours. As the temperature rises the relative brightness of each of the constituent colours changes.

from an object at a given temperature. It was changes in these relative brightnesses as temperature increased that explained why objects went from being red-hot at fairly low temperatures to white-hot or blue-hot at fairly high temperatures (Figure 1.28).

Planck found that, in order to account for the observed pattern of emission from hot bodies, he had to assume that energy was transferred from the heated surface to the emitted radiation in a 'grainy' way. Corresponding to each particular colour of light there was a minimum amount of energy — a *quantum* of energy — that could be carried away from the surface by the light. The size of this quantum of energy depended on the colour of the light; an energy quantum of violet light was almost twice as energetic as an energy quantum of red light, and every other colour had its own charac-teristic quantum. Planck was able to write down a law that related the quantum of energy corresponding to any particular colour to the physical property (frequency) which determined that colour. In doing so he introduced a new fundamental constant of Nature — now called **Planck's constant** ($h = 6.626 \times 10^{-34}$ joule seconds). The appearance of Planck's constant in a calculation can be taken as a clear indication that quantum physics is involved.

Planck's law was used with great success over the following quarter of a century, in a variety of contexts. Einstein used it in his 1905 paper explaining the photoelectric effect, and so did the Danish physicist Niels Bohr (1885–1962), in 1913, when he formulated a theory of the inner workings of the atom that achieved some remarkable successes in spite of a number of unsatisfactory features. It showed up again in 1924 in the doctoral thesis of Louis de Broglie (1892–1987), who suggested that entities which are normally thought of as particles, such as electrons, actually have a wave-like aspect to their behaviour. Einstein, Bohr and de Broglie all received Nobel Prizes in recognition of their work.

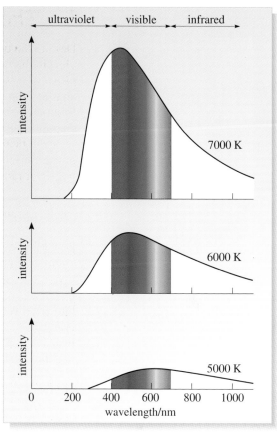

Figure 1.29 Graphs showing the relative intensity of each colour in the light emitted by ideal emitters at different temperatures.

These early developments were strikingly out of step with conventional classical physics. They might even be described as revolutionary, but the real revolution was still to come.

5.1 Quantum mechanics and chance

The real quantum revolution dates from the formulation of **quantum mechanics** by Werner Heisenberg (1901–1976) and others in 1925, and its physical interpretation by Max Born (1882–1970) in 1926. However, before attempting even the most basic sketch of quantum mechanics let's take a small diversion into the realm of philosophy.

The principles of quantum mechanics are discussed in Book 7 and some of its applications are described in Book 8.

The basic working philosophy of most scientists, including those who say they have no philosophy, is a kind of **realism**. (Philosophers recognize many shades of realism.) The three main points of this creed are:

● Our senses allow us to observe a physical world, and our bodies allow us to interact with that world.

● Although our perceptions may differ, we all share the same physical world, which exists independently of our observations, e.g. the same Moon is really out there for all of us, even if none of us is looking at it.

●   Although our actions may cause disturbances, it is possible to investigate the physical world without destroying its essential structure. We may therefore try to deduce the essential features of the physical world by combining experiment and observation with rational speculation.

One of the many astonishing features of quantum mechanics is that it calls into question some of the central ideas of this kind of realist philosophy. When speaking about the nature of the microscopic entities that are described by quantum mechanics one of the subject's pioneers said:

'…they form a world of potentialities or possibilities rather than one of things or facts.'

Werner Heisenberg

Another of the quantum pioneers put it even more simply:

'There is no quantum world.'

Niels Bohr

Let's see how such statements came to be made.

By 1925 it was clear that atoms consisted of positively charged cores, called *nuclei*, around which swarmed negatively charged *electrons*. It was also clear that conventional classical mechanics was incapable of correctly describing the behaviour of those electrons, and the search was on for a new mechanics that could be applied to particles in the atomic domain. The (limited) success of Bohr's model of the atom indicated that the new mechanics would involve Planck's constant, so Max Born, a leading atomic researcher at the University of Göttingen in Germany, named the new mechanics *quantum mechanics*, even though he had no real idea of its basic rules at the time. It was supposed that quantum mechanics would be more fundamental than classical mechanics, so that once the rules of quantum mechanics were uncovered it would be possible to deduce the laws of classical mechanics from them.

Those basic rules of quantum mechanics were actually brought to light over a period of about a year, starting in the summer of 1925. The first breakthrough was made by Werner Heisenberg, a 24-year-old researcher at Göttingen, who had been working closely with Born. Heisenberg's first paper on the subject sketched out his basic ideas, but it was far from being a systematic formulation of quantum mechanics; neither the mathematical basis of quantum mechanics (its *formalism*) nor its physical meaning (its *interpretation*) was at all clear. Intensive work by Heisenberg, Born and others over the next six months did much to clarify the formalism (which turned out to involve mathematical objects called *matrices*), and to show that quantum mechanics was at least as successful as Bohr's rather unsatisfactory atomic theory, but it did not clarify the interpretation. At that stage, early in 1926, Erwin Schrödinger (1887–1961), an Austrian working at the University of Zurich, published a different and somewhat simpler formulation of quantum mechanics. Schrödinger's approach was based on de Broglie's idea that matter has a wave-like aspect. Schrödinger himself soon showed that his approach was mathematically equivalent to that of Heisenberg, but he too had difficulty working out what it all meant.

The key step in the interpretation of quantum mechanics was first put into print by Born in June 1926. Imagine that you could arrange a collision between a particle and a target and that, after the collision, the particle was deflected to the left. If you could repeat the collision under *exactly* the same conditions, you would naturally expect to see the particle deflected to the left again. If the particle were unexpectedly deflected to the right you would probably assume that the second collision had been set up in a slightly different way to the first, in spite of your best efforts to make the conditions identical. Born used the new formalism of quantum mechanics to study collisions and realized that, in utter contrast to classical expectations, *quantum mechanics allows identical experiments to have different outcomes*. Two collisions could be set up in *exactly* the same way (the discreteness of quantum mechanics helps to enable this). Yet, in spite of starting out in the same way, a particle may be deflected to the left in one collision and to the right in the other. In any single collision it is impossible to predict which way the particle will go.

You might wonder whether science is possible at all if Nature behaves so capriciously. Fortunately, quantum mechanics does allow us to make predictions, but with some uncertainty. In any experiment, the formalism of quantum mechanics can, in principle, predict:

● the possible outcomes;

● the **probability** (i.e. the relative likelihood or chance) of each of those possible outcomes.

However, what quantum mechanics cannot do, and what Born was convinced it would never do, was to go beyond probabilities and predict a definite outcome for a particular experiment that might have more than one outcome. Returning to the example of collisions, quantum mechanics can predict that particles colliding in a certain way might be deflected to the left *or* to the right; it can also predict the *probability* of deflection to the left or the right and hence the relative numbers deflected left or right in a large number of identical collisions; but it cannot predict whether a particular particle in a particular collision will be deflected right or left. Dealing with probabilities is an *intrinsic* part of quantum physics that cannot be avoided.

The use of probability in physics was not new. But the suggestion that probability was intrinsic and unavoidable was shocking. In classical physics, probability was used when something which could be known in principle (such as the exact path of a particle) was not known; probability filled the gap left by ignorance. Statistical mechanics, for example, used probabilities to estimate likely pressures and entropies, compensating for ignorance about detailed molecular motions. It was not doubted however, that such details existed, and could be determined in principle. In quantum mechanics the situation was completely different; a probabilistic statement along the lines of 'this has a 30% chance of happening' might well be the *most* that could be said in a certain situation, even in principle.

Niels Bohr, whose atomic theory was overthrown by quantum mechanics, was a keen supporter of the new mechanics. He had partly inspired Heisenberg to undertake its development in the first place, and in May 1926 he welcomed Heisenberg to his institute in Copenhagen where a great deal of effort went into formulating a complete interpretation of quantum mechanics that included the idea of intrinsic probabilities. The **Copenhagen interpretation** that emerged from this work is now regarded as the conventional interpretation of quantum mechanics, though there have always been those who have questioned its correctness. Some of the features of this interpretation are:

● The measurable properties of objects (position, velocity, etc.) do not generally have values except just after a measurement.

● Measurement causes potentiality to become actuality.

● The measured values occur at frequencies determined by probabilistic rules. The probabilities are intrinsic and fundamental, and can be predicted by quantum mechanics.

The last of these points represents a substantial shift from classical determinism. In classical mechanics the past uniquely determines the present and hence the future. In

Figure 1.30 A quantum mechanical model of a hydrogen atom, which has *one* electron, in its state of lowest energy. The varying density of the spots indicates the relative likelihood of finding the electron in any particular region.

quantum mechanics this is not so. Even the most complete possible knowledge of the past would only permit the calculation of the probability of future events. Some, perhaps a little naively, saw in this a scientific basis for free will: there was an element of freedom, or at least of chance, in the Universe.

The Copenhagen interpretation calls simple realism into question. If the most that you can say about a position measurement you are about to perform is that various values may be obtained, with various probabilities, then it may well mean that the object has no position until it is measured. Note that this is quite different from saying that the object has a position which you don't happen to know — it is as if the object had not made up its mind where to appear until the position measurement has been made. Clearly if you say that the object has *no* position, you call into question its independent reality, and hence the philosophy of realism, at least in its simplest form. This emphasizes the enormous importance of measurement in quantum physics and the motivation for making statements such as '… they form a world of potentialities or possibilities rather than one of things or facts' and 'there is no quantum world'.

An alternative stance is to assume that there is a real world out there, but to admit that it cannot be adequately described in terms of classical concepts such as position or velocity. This is plausible. We have no right to expect microscopic physics to be just a scaled-down version of everyday experience. Given that quantum mechanics deals with a microscopic world well beyond the immediate reach of our senses and intuitions, perhaps the most surprising thing is that we can make predictions at all. From this perspective, the price that must be paid for the mismatch between our classical concepts and the quantum world is astonishingly small, and is reflected mainly in the appearance of probabilities. In philosophical terms, the concept of a real world can be preserved by admitting that certain aspects of it are inaccessible to us, clumsy giants that we are. But in practical, or scientific, terms this makes no difference. It is hard to see how we could ever develop an understanding that was not based on classical concepts, so probabilities seem destined to remain intrinsic and unavoidable, offering the only gateway through which we can glimpse the microscopic world.

Question 1.6   In Section 1 it was said that the notion of scientific law was based on the fact that identical situations produced identical outcomes. To what extent does this remain true in quantum physics where identical experiments may produce different outcomes?   ■

5.2 Quantum fields and unification

From its inception, quantum physics was concerned not just with particles such as electrons, but also with light and other forms of electromagnetic radiation. In 1900 Planck discovered the quantum in the transfer of energy from matter to radiation, and in 1905, Einstein's explanation of the photoelectric effect assumed that the transfer of energy from radiation to matter occurred in a similarly quantized fashion. It is therefore hardly surprising that the development of quantum mechanics was soon followed by an attempt to formulate a quantum theory of electromagnetic radiation. That meant, of course, combining quantum ideas such as Planck's constant and intrinsic probabilities with the field theory of electromagnetism. The result would be a **quantum field theory**.

The quantum field theory of electromagnetism is called **quantum electrodynamics**, or QED for short. Its formulation proved to be very difficult. The first steps were taken by the British physicist Paul Dirac in 1927, but the theory was not really sorted out until the late 1940s.

Paul Adrien Maurice Dirac (1902–1984)

Paul Adrien Maurice Dirac was born in Bristol, England, in 1902. His father was a Swiss-born teacher of French, his mother a librarian. Dirac's first degree, obtained at the Merchant Venturer's Technical College, was in electrical engineering, but he had no real interest in the subject and after graduating spent two years studying mathematics at the University of Bristol. In 1923 he left Bristol for Cambridge where he remained for most of his working life.

Dirac's achievements in Cambridge were prodigious. In 1925, while working for his doctorate, he became one of the founders of quantum mechanics when he produced an elegant extension of Heisenberg's work. A little over a year later he presented a very general formulation of quantum mechanics that has remained the basis of the subject ever since. During the next year he essentially founded quantum electrodynamics. In 1928 Dirac took an important step towards bringing quantum physics into conformity with Einstein's special theory of relativity by devising an equation (now called the Dirac equation) that could describe the behaviour of electrons at any speed up to the speed of light. This equation provided a natural explanation of one of the electron's intrinsic properties — its spin. Taking the mathematical form of his equation seriously, and searching for a way of interpreting it, Dirac was led, in 1931, to propose that there should exist a class of 'anti-electrons', particles with the same mass and spin as the electron but with the opposite electrical charge (Figure 1.32). By correctly predicting the existence of these antiparticles, now called positrons, Dirac became recognized as the 'discoverer' of antimatter — one of the most important discoveries of the century.

From 1932 to 1969 Dirac held the Lucasian Chair of Mathematics in Cambridge, the post that Newton himself had once occupied. During this period Dirac

Figure 1.31   Paul Dirac.

worked on a variety of topics including *magnetic monopoles* (hypothetical magnetic charges) and the speculation that the fundamental constants of physics might be gradually changing in a co-ordinated way. However he became disenchanted with some of the detailed developments that occurred in quantum field theory and became increasingly distanced from what others regarded as the scientific mainstream.

In 1971, following his retirement from Cambridge, Dirac moved to the USA where he became a professor of physics at Florida State University. He died there in 1984. Throughout his life Dirac was renowned for his economy of speech and lack of social awareness. His book *Principles of Quantum Mechanics* (1930) is regarded as a classic of clear and elegant exposition. When a correspondent asked him to clarify a certain result in the text, Dirac is said to have replied that he knew of no clearer way of expressing the point. No rudeness would have been intended, just an honest statement of fact. Dirac preferred to work by himself, and had few collaborators or research students.

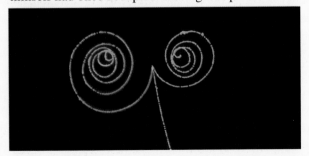
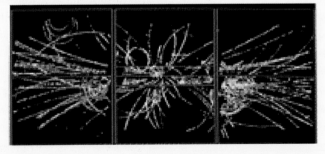

Figure 1.32   Tracks left by fundamental particles. (a) An electron and a positron (a particle–antiparticle pair) reveal their opposite charges by spiralling in different directions in a magnetic field. (b) A variety of particles created from the energy released when an electron and a positron collide at high speed and annihilate.

During the lengthy development of QED the following important features of quantum field theory became apparent.

- *Quantum field theory provides the natural way of combining special relativity and quantum physics.* Quantum mechanics, as originally formulated by Heisenberg and Schrödinger was inconsistent with the principle of relativity. Attempts were made to rectify this problem and significant progress was made by Dirac with his relativistic electron equation. However, despite many successes it became increasingly clear that relativistic quantum mechanics was ultimately self-contradictory and that quantum field theory provided the natural way of producing a relativistic quantum physics.

- *Quantum fields may be regarded as collections of particles.* In the case of the quantized electromagnetic field these particles are called **photons**. Each photon of a particular colour carries a characteristic amount of energy: the quantum of energy used by Planck and Einstein. Emission and absorption of radiation corresponds to the creation and destruction of photons and therefore inevitably involves the transfer of complete quanta of energy. (Interestingly, Einstein realized as early as 1905 that the quantized transfer of energy would be explained if radiation actually consisted of particles, but the idea was not well received and he did not press it. Photons only became an accepted part of physics in the 1920s.)

- *Quantum field theory can be used to describe all fundamental particles.* Electrons and positrons are normally regarded as examples of fundamental particles of matter. In quantum field theory all such particles are associated with quantum fields in much the same way that photons are associated with the electromagnetic field. The number of particles of a given type reflects the state of excitation of the field, and the particles are said to be 'quanta of excitation' of the field. Thus, although quantum field theory describes particles and the forces between them, it does so entirely in terms of quantum fields.

- *Quantum field theory describes processes in which particles are created or destroyed.* When a quantum field becomes more excited, the number of quanta of excitation increases. This occurs because new particle–antiparticle pairs are created from radiation. When a quantum field becomes less excited, the number of quanta of excitation decreases. This is achieved by processes in which particles and antiparticles collide and annihilate one another to produce radiation. (Both of these processes are permitted by Einstein's $E = mc^2$, and were explicitly predicted by Dirac.)

These were all very attractive features of quantum field theory and raised the hope that it might be a truly fundamental theory capable of providing a new world-view. However there were serious problems within quantum electrodynamics that had to be overcome before such hopes stood any chance of being realized. Using QED to predict the value of a physically measurable quantity involved, in practice, working out the contribution made by several different sub-processes. Making sure that these sub-processes were fully identified was a problem in itself, working out their individual contributions was even worse. Even in the simplest cases determining the contributions was difficult, and in the more complicated cases the result was usually a meaningless infinity showing that something was wrong. It was the problem of infinities that really delayed the completion of QED until the late 1940s. At that time, in a burst of post-war activity, a technique called *renormalization* was developed that made it possible to get at the physical result hidden behind the unphysical infinity. At the same time a simple diagrammatic method was devised that made it much easier to identify and perform the necessary calculations. The problem of infinities was solved by Julian Schwinger (1918–1994), Sin-itiro Tomonaga (1906–1979) and Richard P. Feynman. The last of these was also responsible for the diagrams, which have become known as *Feynman diagrams* (Figure 1.33).

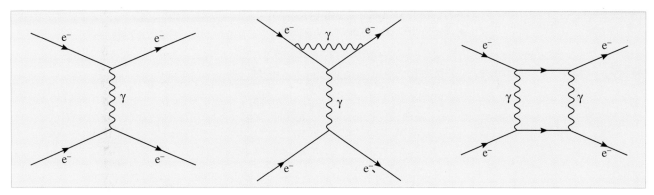

Figure 1.33 Feynman diagrams of some of the processes that contribute to the scattering of colliding electrons. Each diagram represents a complicated mathematical expression. The wavy lines represent photons.

Richard P. Feynman (1918–1988)

Figure 1.34 Richard P. Feynman.

Richard Phillips Feynman was one of the most colourful and celebrated of US physicists. He was born in New York in 1918 and educated at the Massachusetts Institute of Technology (MIT) and Princeton. From 1942 to 1945 he was involved in the atomic bomb project at Los Alamos, where he gave ample evidence of his enormous technical virtuosity as well as earning himself a reputation as a practical joker.

After the Second World War Feynman went to Cornell University where he became one of the major figures in the development of quantum electrodynamics (QED). During this period he also devised his own

approach to quantum mechanics called the 'path integral' or 'sum over histories' approach. This has since been applied to quantum field theory and is now the standard formalism in many areas of the subject.

In 1950 Feynman moved to the California Institute of Technology (Caltech) where he remained for the rest of his life. While there, he worked on many topics, including the theory of fundamental particles, the theory of superfluidity and the nature of the forces and interactions within the atomic nucleus. He became renowned as a teacher of physics, combining profound physical insight with a very down-to-earth style. Towards the end of his life, when already ill with cancer, he was invited to join the commission investigating the in-flight explosion of the space shuttle *Challenger*. As part of that work he memorably demonstrated, in front of a massive TV audience, the disastrous effect of low temperature on the booster rocket's O-ring seals by dropping one of them into a glass of iced water.

Feynman will long be remembered as one of the twentieth century's greatest exponents of intuitive — yet highly rigorous — physics. The three volumes of *Feynman Lectures on Physics* from his Caltech years, and Feynman's autobiographical works 'Surely You're Joking Mr Feynman!' and 'What Do You Care What Other People Think?' also ensure that he will be remembered as a character of extraordinary insight, wit and charm. In 1965 Feynman shared the Nobel Prize for Physics with Julian Schwinger and Sin-itiro Tomonaga.

The completion of QED presented physicists with the most precise theory of Nature they had ever possessed. However, by the time that completion had been achieved it was already clear that electromagnetism and gravitation were not the only forces at work in the world. The familiar contact forces you feel when pressing on a surface had long been understood to be nothing more than manifestations of electromagnetism — atoms repelling other atoms that got too close — but the 1930s and 1940s had provided clear evidence of the existence of two other fundamental forces. These new forces were quite powerful, but both were of such short range that they mainly operated within atoms rather than between them. The new forces were called the **strong** and **weak nuclear forces** since their effects were most clearly seen in the behaviour of atomic nuclei. The major properties of all four of the fundamental forces are listed in Table 1.1.

Table 1.1 The four fundamental forces. The strengths are roughly those found at high collision energies, and the force carriers are the particles most closely associated with each force. The graviton is followed by a question mark because its existence is still in doubt.

Force	Strength	Range	Force carrier
strong	10^{-1}	10^{-15} m	gluon
electromagnetic	10^{-2}	infinite	photon
weak	10^{-2}	10^{-17} m	W and Z bosons
gravitational	10^{-45}	infinite	graviton(?)

Formulating quantum field theories of each of the four fundamental forces was an obvious goal, and remains so to this day. Three of the forces — the strong, the weak and the electromagnetic — have been treated with great success; and have been combined to form a so-called *standard model* of fundamental forces. However, gravity has resisted all attempts to fit it into the same kind of theoretical strait-jacket and seems to require very special treatment if it is to be treated as a quantum field theory at all. If it were not for the problem of gravity we would be able to say that the physicist's current world-view is that the Universe consists of a set of mutually interacting quantum fields that fill the space-time described by special relativity. But it seems that this will not do.

A way forward may be indicated by the standard model itself. The standard model is actually something more than a description of three of the four fundamental forces; it is also to some extent a prototype for their union. Within the standard model the electromagnetic and weak forces appear as a unified electroweak force. The exact meaning of **unification** in this context is too technical to go into here, but suffice it to say that, under unification, the quantum fields responsible for the weak and electromagnetic forces combine in a way that is slightly reminiscent of Einstein's fusion of space and time to form space-time.

The success of electroweak unification has been one of the motivations for suggesting that all three of the forces that appear in the standard model might be unified within a grand unified theory, and that a further step of unification might also incorporate gravity, thus bringing all four fundamental forces within a single *superunified* theory. The form that such a superunified theory might take is far from clear. Would it involve quantum fields in a curved space-time, or would something altogether more radical be required?

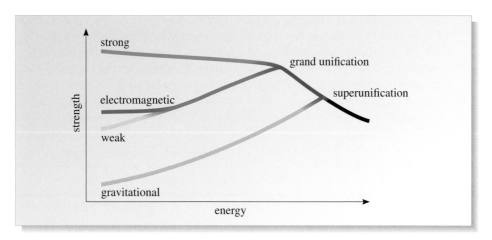

Figure 1.35 A possible route to superunification of the four fundamental forces. At low energies we have laboratory evidence of four forces, but the weak and electromagnetic forces are known to acquire a common strength at high energies. Perhaps this process continues.

For some time many hoped that an approach called *string theory* might provide a solution to the problem of superunification. The idea of this approach was that the basic entities were not quantized fields that filled the points of four-dimensional space-time, but rather extended objects called *strings* that vibrated in ten or more dimensions. There was never any experimental evidence to support this idea, but what really caused theorists to lose faith in it was the discovery that string theory is not unique. There is a strong prejudice amongst those searching for a unified theory of everything that there should only be one such theory, not a whole class of them. String theory fails to satisfy this uniqueness criterion. However, hope of string-based superunification has not been entirely lost. A new subject called *M-theory* is being investigated in which all of the plausible string theories appear as different aspects of a single theory — perhaps.

At the present time, the quest to find the ultimate constituents of the Universe and the laws that regulate their behaviour ends not with an answer, but with a set of loose ends. Perhaps this is as it should be in a healthy science, or perhaps it is a sign that we are heading towards a dead end. Perhaps there is no single world-view for physics to uncover, or perhaps it is not the function of physics to do so.

Question 1.7 Does quantum field theory suffer from the same kind of conflict with simple realism that arose in quantum mechanics? ■

5.3 The end of physics?

Suppose for the moment that quantum field theory, or string theory or M-theory, or some other theory no one has yet heard of, does turn out to be the much sought-after superunified theory. Suppose it is unique and is so wonderfully compact that it can be printed on the front of a teeshirt. What would such a theory really tell us about the world?

Looking on the positive side, the theory should indicate the fundamental entities of which the world is composed, whether they are particles, strings, quantum fields, or whatever. The theory should also indicate the truly fundamental constants of Nature (it may be that Planck's constant, the speed of light and so on are not really as fundamental as we think), and it should certainly indicate all the fundamental processes that can occur — the elementary processes from which all other processes are composed. This would be the ultimate realization of **reductionism**, the view that every phenomenon can be reduced to some more elementary set of phenomena, all the way back to a set of truly fundamental entities and interactions.

Being rather more negative, a fundamental theory of everything might not really tell us very much at all. It is hard to believe, for example, that even a supremely intelligent scientist equipped with as much computing power as he or she could desire could set to work from the theory of everything and predict the existence of the Earth, let alone something like my choice of breakfast today. They might show that the existence of an Earth-like planet, or an egg-like breakfast was *consistent* with the theory of everything, but that's a long way from predicting particular cases. There are several reasons why a theory of everything will probably not really be a theory of all that much. Here are some:

- *The problem of initial conditions.* In a fully deterministic theory, such as Newtonian mechanics, the present is determined by the past. To predict particular eventualities in the present Universe we would therefore need to know the initial state of our Universe. It may not be impossible to determine these cosmic initial conditions, but it's not clear, and it is hard to believe we will ever know for sure.

- *The problem of indeterminacy.* We have seen that when it comes to predicting particular events quantum physics is limited to making probabilistic predictions. It seems certain that quantum physics will be an underlying principle of any conceivable theory of everything, so the predictions may always be limited to possibilities rather than particular eventualities. Some might hope, as Einstein did, that quantum physics will eventually be shown to be incomplete and that a full theory will replace probability by certainty, but all current indications are that this is not going to be the case and the one thing that's certain is that uncertainty is here to stay.

- *The problem of emergence.* Reductionism was originally a biological doctrine which aimed to reduce biology to more fundamental sciences such as chemistry and physics. It was opposed by the doctrine of **emergence** which claimed that even if all physical and chemical phenomena were known it would not be possible to predict biological phenomena because new properties emerged at the level of biology that were not contained in any of its parts. These doctrines are now used generally in discussions of science, including physics. To give a physical example; water is wet and it is made of molecules, yet no molecule is wet; the wetness is a property of the water that emerges when large numbers of molecules come together. Most physicists would expect a satisfactory explanation of the wetness of water to make contact with fundamental principles (somehow, the wetness of water must be implicit in the electrical interactions of its molecules) and, in this sense, they are reductionists. But it often happens that complex phenomena require explanations on many different levels, and it would be wrong to dismiss the higher levels as being unimportant, or uninteresting to the physicist. The interactions of atoms and molecules are now understood — at least in terms of the fundamental laws that operate. Yet a wealth of unexpected phenomena continues to emerge in the physics of atoms, molecules, solids and liquids, showing that there is much to explore in physics above the most fundamental level. The challenges are as much to do with understanding the consequences of known laws as with discovering new ones. Perhaps the ultimate challenge will be to provide a chain of understanding that links fundamental principles to truly complex phenomena, such as how a brain works.

For all of these reasons, and others you can discover for yourself, it seems safe to conclude that physics has a healthy future that might well include a theory of everything, but which is very unlikely to be ended by such a theory.

6 Closing items

6.1 Chapter summary

1   Laws summarize regularities observed in Nature. They can summarize large numbers of similar phenomena and make it possible to predict the course of particular phenomena.

2   In physics, many of the laws are expressed mathematically and concern measurable quantities. This aids precision and clarity, and it supports rational argument.

3   Newtonian mechanics is based on equations (Newton's laws of motion, Newton's law of universal gravitation) that are deterministic: they have the property that the present is entirely determined by the past. Complete knowledge of the state of the Universe at any one time would make possible, in principle, the determination of its state at all other times.

4   Thermodynamics, with its emphasis on energy conservation (the first law) and entropy growth (the second law) indicates an effectively unavoidable irreversibility in the laws of Nature.

5   Electromagnetism was ultimately responsible for the introduction of the field as a new fundamental ingredient in physical world-views. Although attempts were made to formulate mechanical models of the electromagnetic field, such efforts are no longer a serious topic of scientific investigation. Fields are introduced to avoid the use of action at a distance.

6   Special relativity is based on the idea that observers in uniform motion should agree about the laws of physics. It has the effect of unifying space and time into a space-time that different observers slice into space and time in ways that depend on their relative motion.

7   General relativity represents gravity as a manifestation of space-time curvature: 'matter tells space how to curve, space tells matter how to move'.

8   Quantum physics is characterized by the intrinsic and unavoidable use of probability (implying indeterminacy in the behaviour of individual systems). Quantum mechanics is a major subdivision of quantum physics that deals with particles and calls into question the simplest kind of realism. Quantum field theory is another major subdivision of quantum physics. It deals with fields and represents a natural fusion of quantum physics and special relativity. Quantum fields can be interpreted in terms of particles and provide a good way of describing at least three of the four fundamental forces of Nature.

6.2 Achievements

Now that you have completed this chapter, you should be able to:

A1 Explain the meaning of all the newly defined (emboldened) terms introduced in this chapter.

A2 Explain what is meant by a physical world-view and describe some of the major world-views that have emerged during the evolution of physics.

A3 Describe some of the major concepts of physics, give brief biographical sketches of some of the major contributors to the development of physics and name some of the major events that have helped to shape the subject.

A4 Comment on some of the philosophical issues that are raised by the study of physics.

After using the multimedia package, you should also be able to:

A5 Install and run the multimedia package, and carry out the actions required by it.

6.3 End-of-chapter questions

Question 1.8 Express the following numbers using scientific (powers of ten) notation: (a) 2.1 million, (b) 36 000, (c) 1/10, (d) 0.000 05.

Question 1.9 List the major revolutions in physics that have occurred since 1650. Describe each in one or two sentences, giving only enough detail to distinguish it from the others.

Question 1.10 Describe the concept of a field. Briefly outline the history of this concept from the time of Faraday to the present day.

Question 1.11 Briefly describe the opposition that exists between reductionism and emergence.

Question 1.12 On the basis of dates of birth and death alone, which of the following pairs of physicists might have been able to meet for a discussion about their scientific discoveries?

(a) Galileo and Newton

(b) Newton and Laplace

(c) Laplace and Coulomb

(d) Coulomb and Faraday

(e) Faraday and Maxwell

(f) Maxwell and Einstein

(g) Einstein and Bohr

(h) Bohr and Heisenberg

(i) Heisenberg and Dirac ■

Appendix: Some highlights of physics

c. 624 BC	Birth of Thales of Miletus; traditionally 'the first physicist'.
384 BC	Birth of Aristotle; author of *Physics*.
1543	Nicolaus Copernicus' *De Revolutionibus Orbium Celestium*.
1600	William Gilbert's *De Magnete* describing the behaviour of magnets.
1609	Johannes Kepler's first and second laws published in *Astronomia Nova*.
1632	Galileo's *Dialogue Concerning the Two Chief Systems of the World* published.
1638	Galileo's work on motion described in his *Discorsi*.
1687	Newton's laws of motion and gravitation published in his *Principia*.
1704	Newton's work on light and spectra described in his *Opticks*.
1729	Stephen Gray discovers electrical conduction.
1736	Leonhard Euler introduces differential equations into mechanics.
1755	Euler lays the foundations of fluid mechanics.
1784	Pierre Laplace introduces concept of electric potential.
1785	Charles Coulomb announces his law of electrostatics.
1799	Pierre Laplace's *Méchanique Céleste* (Volume 1).
1801	Thomas Young demonstrates the wave nature of light.
1803	John Dalton proposes his atomic theory of matter.
1820	Hans Oersted demonstrates electromagnetism.
1821	Michael Faraday demonstrates the principle of the electric motor.
1825	Sadi Carnot lays the foundations of thermodynamics.
1843	James Joule determines the mechanical equivalent of heat.
1847	Hermann von Helmholtz formulates conservation of energy.
1848	Lord Kelvin proposes the absolute temperature scale.
1849	Armand Fizeau makes first accurate measurement of the speed of light.
1850	Rudolf Clausius introduces entropy.
1859	James Clerk Maxwell develops the kinetic theory of gases.
1865	Maxwell's *Dynamical Theory of the Electromagnetic Field*.
1871	Dmitry Mendeleev's periodic table of the elements.
1877	Ludwig Boltzmann introduces statistical interpretation of entropy.
1882	Albert Michelson measures the speed of light.
1887	Michelson–Morley experiment fails to detect the ether.
1887	Heinrich Hertz discovers photoelectric effect.
1888	Heinrich Hertz demonstrates the existence of radio waves.
1895	Wilhelm Röntgen discovers X-rays.
1896	Henri Becquerel discovers radioactivity.
1897	J. J. Thomson discovers the electron.

1900	Max Planck introduces the quantum.
1905	Einstein publishes papers on special relativity, Brownian motion and the photoelectric effect.
1911	Ernest Rutherford announces discovery of the atomic nucleus.
1911	Victor Hess discovers cosmic rays.
1913	Niels Bohr's quantum theory of the atom.
1916	Einstein's general theory of relativity.
1924	Bose–Einstein statistics introduced.
1925	Heisenberg introduces quantum mechanics (matrix form).
1925	Wolfgang Pauli announces the exclusion principle.
1926	Schrödinger introduces wave mechanics.
1926	Born's probability interpretation of quantum mechanics.
1926	Fermi–Dirac statistics introduced.
1927	Heisenberg formulates the uncertainty principle.
1928	The Dirac equation describes relativistic electrons and leads to an understanding of spin and the prediction of antiparticles.
1929	Edwin Hubble discovers the expansion of the Universe.
1932	James Chadwick discovers the neutron.
1932	Carl Anderson discovers the positron.
1934	Fermi introduces the weak interaction.
1935	Hideki Yukawa lays the foundation of the strong interaction.
1939	Otto Hahn and Lise Meitner discover nuclear fission.
1948	John Bardeen, William Brattain and William Shockley produce the transistor.
1948	Feynman introduces his diagrams for quantum electrodynamics.
1948	George Gamow proposes the basis of Big Bang theory.
1964	Murray Gell-Mann introduces quarks.
1965	Arno Penzias and Robert Wilson discover cosmic microwave background radiation.
1967	Jocelyn Bell Burnell discovers first pulsar (a neutron star).
1968	Steven Weinberg, Abdus Salam and Sheldon Glashow develop unified theory of electroweak interaction.
1972	Fritsch, Gell-Mann and Bardeen develop quantum chromodynamics.
1977	Klaus von Klitzing discovers the quantum Hall effect.
1980	Alan Guth proposes an inflationary early Universe.
1981	Green and Schwarz introduce superstring theory.
1982	Alain Aspect conducts experiment demonstrating non-local aspects of quantum physics.
1986	Bednorz and Mueller discover high-temperature superconductivity.
1991	CERN confirms the existence of three generations of fundamental particles.
1995	Witten and Townsend develop M-Theory.
1995	Cornell, Wieman and Anderson discover Bose–Einstein condensate of atomic gas.

Suggestions for further reading

If you wish to pursue some of the topics discussed in this book in greater detail you might like to start with one or other of the following works.

General

John D. Barrow (1988), *The World Within the World*, Oxford.

Richard P. Feynman (1992), *The Character of Physical Law*, Penguin Books.

Brian Greene (1999), *The Elegant Universe*, W. W. Norton.

Werner Heisenberg (1990), *Physics and Philosophy*, Penguin Books.

Jan Hilgevoord (ed.) (1994), *Physics and our view of the world*, Cambridge.

Steven Weinberg (1993), *Dreams of a final theory*, Vintage.

Historical

William Berkson (1974), *Fields of Force*, RKP.

I. Bernard Cohen (1987), *The Birth of a New Physics*, Penguin.

P. M. Harman (1982), *Energy, Force and Matter*, Cambridge.

Abraham Pais (1986), *Inward Bound*, Oxford.

Christopher Ray (1987), *The Evolution of Relativity*, Adam Hilger.

Silvan S. Schweber (1994), *QED and the men who made it*, Princeton.

Emilio Segrè (1980), *From X-rays to Quarks*, Freeman.

Emilio Segrè (1984), *From Falling Bodies to Radio Waves*, Freeman.

Biographical

On Heisenberg: D. C. Cassidy (1992), *Uncertainty*, New York.

Richard P. Feynman (1985), '*Surely You're Joking Mr. Feynman!*', Unwin.

David Gooding and Frank James (eds.) (1985), *Faraday Rediscovered*, Stockton.

Helge Kragh (1990), *Dirac*, Cambridge.

Walter Moore (1992), *Schrödinger*, Cambridge.

On Einstein: Abraham Pais (1982), *Subtle is the Lord*, Oxford.

Ivan Tolstoy (1981), *James Clerk Maxwell*, University of Chicago Press.

On Newton: Richard S. Westfall (1980), *Never at Rest*, Cambridge.

Answers and comments

Q1.1 The Chinese were perhaps right, but their complaint is more about language than substance. When we talk about a system obeying a scientific law, we do not mean that the system has understood the law and is consciously following it. We just mean that the behaviour of the system follows a pattern that is predictable, and that someone has discovered and announced this pattern as a scientific law.

Q1.2 *This question is unusually open-ended, with no single correct answer. In preparing our answer we have taken the opportunity to expand the discussion slightly, but would not expect you to include all the points listed below.*

There are several reasons why it would be impossible, in practice, to follow through the Newtonian programme of predicting the entire future of the Universe.

(i) We would need to know the positions and velocities of all the particles in the Universe at a given instant. Nowadays we know that the Universe contains an immense number of fundamental particles. The visible Universe contains about 10^{80} protons and the same number of electrons. Measuring the positions and velocities of such a large number of particles is an unimaginable task. (Indeed, there may be some regions of the Universe that are so remote that we cannot yet know of their existence because the Universe is too young for light from them to have reached us!)

(ii) In order to predict the *exact* future of the Universe, we would need to know the *exact* initial positions and velocities of all the particles. Small errors in measurement may, at first, produce only small errors in prediction, but the errors are cumulative and will eventually become serious. (Nowadays we know that some simple systems are extremely sensitive to the initial conditions. In some cases, it is impossible to measure the initial conditions accurately enough to make anything more than a very short-term prediction. Such systems are said to be *chaotic*. They will be discussed more fully in Book 3.)

(iii) We need to know all the forces acting between particles. Newton only produced an explicit formula for gravitational forces. His work was later extended to cover electromagnetic forces, but our understanding of the interactions between particles remains partial and a complete understanding elusive.

(iv) Even if we had all the information necessary, the calculations would be far too difficult to carry out. No computer could ever attempt an exact solution. And even if the calculations could be done, there would be nowhere to store all the results.

For all these reasons, we cannot hope to predict the exact future of the Universe. That would be too much to expect. The great successes of physics emerge when we ask specific questions about systems that are simple, or can be thought of as being simple, so that the mathematical analysis remains feasible for humans and their computers.

Q1.3 By the second law of thermodynamics, the total entropy of the Universe must not decrease. The entropy of warm objects placed inside the fridge decreases as heat flows from them. At the same time, the back of the fridge is warm, so the surroundings of the fridge are warmed and their entropy is increased. The second law of thermodynamics is satisfied because the increase in entropy of the surroundings of the fridge is equal or greater in magnitude than the decrease in entropy of the fridge contents.

Q1.4 Electromagnetic waves are predicted by Maxwell's equations, as disturbances of Faraday's electric and magnetic fields. The disturbances travel at the speed of light, which is finite. Thus Faraday's idea that disturbances of fields should travel at a finite speed was confirmed.

Q1.5 According to special relativity, different observers disagree about how to slice space-time up into space and time. But observers are not free to make *arbitrary* choices. All observers must find that light travels at a constant speed of $c = 2.998 \times 10^8$ metres per second, and this will not be possible if an observer uses a clock that is running slower and slower, for example. The definition of time is made quite naturally in special relativity as the time ticked on a regularly running clock that travels with the observer.

Q1.6 In quantum mechanics, identical situations do not always produce identical outcomes. Nevertheless, a certain regularity remains because if an experimental arrangement has a variety of possible outcomes, each occurring with a definite probability, subsequent repetitions of the experiment will have the same outcomes occurring with the same probabilities. By repeating the experiment a large number of times we can check whether the probabilities predicted by quantum mechanics are valid. The most important characteristic of a scientific law is that it should be open to experimental tests. Quantum mechanics has introduced a new type of scientific law — one based on probability which embraces the fact that identical situations do not produce identical outcomes.

Q1.7 Quantum field theory is based on the idea of intrinsic probability, just as ordinary quantum mechanics is. It therefore raises exactly the same questions about simple realism.

Q1.8 (a) 2.1×10^6; (b) 3.6000×10^4; (c) 1.0×10^{-1}; (d) 5×10^{-5}. Each of these answers assumes a certain level of precision. For example, 2.1 million has been interpreted as 2.1 million, rather than 2.2 million, so only two digits have been retained in scientific notation; 36 000 has been interpreted as 36 000 rather than 36 001, and this greater precision is indicated by using five digits.

Q1.9 (i) Newtonian mechanics explained the motion of particles in terms of the forces acting on them. The law of gravitation illustrated how forces could be calculated, while Newton's laws of motion showed how forces influence the motion of particles.

(ii) Thermodynamics deals with processes involving energy transfers, including heat, and clarifies ideas about equilibrium and irreversibility.

(iii) Statistical mechanics interprets thermodynamics in terms of the statistical behaviour of a large number of particles.

(iv) Electromagnetism deals with electricity and magnetism. It replaced the concept of action at a distance by that of a field, and showed that electric and magnetic fields have their own dynamics, leading to the interpretation of light and radio waves as electromagnetic waves.

(v) Special relativity is based on the idea that all observers in uniform motion should agree about the laws of physics. When the laws of electromagnetism were included, this led to a revolution in our ideas of space and time, which were merged together into space-time. Different observers, in different states of uniform motion, disagree about which events are simultaneous in space-time.

(vi) General relativity grew from the desire to express physical laws in the same way for all observers, even those who were not moving uniformly. It became a theory of gravity in which the motion of bodies was determined by the curvature of space-time, caused by sources of gravitation.

(vii) Quantum mechanics describes systems of particles in the atomic domain. It asserts that the fundamental laws of physics involve probability in an intrinsic and unavoidable way, and so casts doubt on simple realism.

(viii) Quantum field theory extends the ideas of quantum mechanics and special relativity to fields. Particles are interpreted as quanta of excitation of the field and may be created or annihilated as the field becomes more or less excited.

Q1.10 A field is a physical quantity with a value at each point in space. A particle passing through a given point will experience forces that depend on the fields at that point. Thus the concept of a field replaces action at a distance.

Faraday introduced fields in the context of magnetism and electricity, and Maxwell established the reality of these fields by showing that wave-like disturbances of electric and magnetic fields can travel through space at the speed of light. He interpreted light as an electromagnetic wave and predicted the existence of longer wavelength electromagnetic waves (radio waves). Einstein's general theory of relativity is a field theory of gravitation in which the field describes the curvature of space-time.

A quantum theory of fields was developed which incorporates ideas from quantum mechanics and special relativity. Quantum electrodynamics is an example of a quantum field theory, in which the electromagnetic field is quantized and the quanta are photons. Quantum field theory also applies to ordinary matter — there are electron fields for example, with the quanta interpreted as the electrons. In quantum field theory, quanta may be created or destroyed as the field becomes more or less excited.

Q1.11 Reductionism is an attempt to interpret everything in terms of fundamental phenomena. For a physicist, this implies trying to explain everything in terms of fundamental particles and their interactions.

Emergence stresses the fact that certain phenomena arise only in complex systems, and have no direct counterpart in terms of fundamental phenomena. For example, an iron bar has a strength that is not directly related to the strength of iron atoms.

Most physicists believe that everything can be related, in principle, to fundamental phenomena. In principle, the strength of an iron bar can be explained in terms of the forces between atoms, which in turn can be explained in terms of quantum field theory. The hard-line reductionist might therefore dismiss the strength of the rod as being of minor importance, since it is a consequence of more fundamental ideas. Most physicists (and even more engineers) would disagree. Advocates of emergence delight in the fact that new phenomena, such as rigidity, emerge from more basic laws. Far from dismissing ideas such as rigidity they use them as valid concepts in their own right.

Q1.12 Laplace and Coulomb, Faraday and Maxwell, Einstein and Bohr, Bohr and Heisenberg, and Heisenberg and Dirac could have met for a discussion of their scientific views. The other pairs either did not overlap, or did not overlap sufficiently for a meaningful scientific discussion to have been possible.

Acknowledgements

Grateful acknowledgement is made to the following sources for permission to reproduce material in this book:

Front cover – Science Museum/Science & Society Picture Library;

Fig. 0.1 COBE – NASA Goddard Space Flight Center and the COBE Science Working Group; COMA cluster of galaxies – NASA & AURA/STSc1; The Spiral Galaxy M83 – Anglo-Australian Observatory, Photograph by David Malin; The Earth's Atmosphere – NASA; Landsat photo of the Wash – Science Photo Library; Whole body picture of A. Einstein – Rijksmuseum; Integrated circuit – Science Photo Library; Ring of 48 Iron atoms – Courtesy of Don Eigler, IBM Research Division; Subatomic particle tracks – CERN/Science Photo Library. *Fig. 0.2* Courtesy of Dana Berry.

Fig. 1.1 Mansell/TimeInc./Katz; *Fig 1.2* Graham Read; *Fig. 1.3a* British Library; *Fig. 1.3b* Science Museum/Science and Society Picture Library; *Fig. 1.6* Mary Evans; *Fig. 1.7* The National Trust Photographic Library/Tessa Musgrave; *Fig. 1.8* British Library; *Fig. 1.9* By permission of the Syndics of Cambridge University Library; *Fig. 1.10* Science Museum/Science & Society Picture Library; *Fig. 1.12a* J. M. Petit Publibphoto Diffusion Science Photo Library; *Fig. 1.13* Science Museum/ Science & Society Picture Library; *Fig. 1.15* Every effort has been made to trace the copyright holder. The publisher will be pleased to make the necessary arrangements at the first opportunity; *Fig. 1.17*, *Fig. 1.18*, *Fig. 1.19*, *Fig. 1.21*, all Science Museum/Science & Society Picture Library; *Fig 1.24* Brian Steadman; *Fig. 1.25* Hulton Getty; *Fig. 1.26* The British Museum; *Fig. 1.27* By permission of Times Newspapers Limited, Copyright Times Newspapers Limited, 1919; *Fig. 1.31* Portrait by Michael Noakes, St John's College Cambridge; *Fig. 1.32a* Lawrence Berkeley Laboratory/Science Photo Library; *Fig. 1.32b* CERN; *Fig. 1.34* Courtesy of the Archives California Institute of Technology.

Index

Entries and page numbers in **bold type** refer to key words which are printed in **bold** in the text and which are defined in the Glossary. These are terms which we expect you to be able to explain the meaning of, and use correctly, both during and at the end of the course.